YAËL DAYAN
Israel Journal: June, 1967

McGRAW-HILL BOOK COMPANY

New York   Toronto   London   Sydney

YAËL DAYAN
Israel Journal: June, 1967

Library of Congress Catalog Card Number: 67-30301

First Edition   16172

The division suffered 240 casualties. Of those 58 dead.

For the sake of accuracy and authenticity I have chosen to write about one division which fought in the Sinai in the 1967 Israeli–Arab war. I was attached to General Sharon's division for a month, and most of the material in this book is based on a diary I kept during this period. I fully believe that the atmosphere, moods, and characteristics of this division reflect those of the whole army before, during, and after the war.

I am grateful to the commanders and soldiers who found the time and patience in the midst of battle and when the war was over to explain to me, talk, and guide me. Special thanks are due to Dov, now my husband, without whom this book would not have been completed.

August, 1967

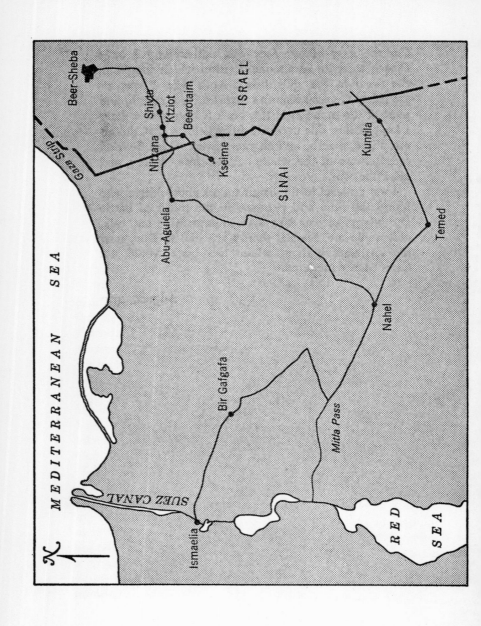

The Week Before

First and foremost there was the loess, a yellowish-gray loam dust raised like a screen to separate all that was from all that was to be. The station wagon pulled up at the check post. I took my small bag and waited for the cloud of dust to recede. When it did, I faced my new home. It was Saturday morning, May 27, and all that was "north" had been hurriedly left behind—Paris, Rome, Athens—the cable home, the BEA flight to Lydda, my unit, empty Tel-Aviv, the road to Beer-Sheba, the road south, then west toward the Egyptian frontier; and now Shivta, division headquarters. Camouflaged vehicles merged into the hill slopes and my sandaled feet sank deep and comfortably in the powdery soil. Small yellow signs indicated directions and I found my way to the war room. The contrast between the word "war room" and its contents reminded me of everything our army stood for: barbed wire, a military policeman, three trucks supporting a tent. I was let in after a short discussion. A pretty blonde called Zipi offered me a cup of coffee. The helicopter pilot, Zeev, was lounging on a camp bed and a small transistor offered us the Hit Parade. Large wooden frames held colorful maps, the communication

1

system was located on the left, and on one of the trucks a few officers were discussing defense plans, the last news bulletin, transportation problems, and the like. For the first few minutes the talk was utterly strange to me. Army jargon, abbreviations, initials, numbers, unfamiliar names, long-forgotten terms. Officers were all addressed by their first names, each had a revolver and a water bottle attached to his belt; they wore high boots and their faces were already tanned and covered with a thick layer of dust which during the weeks that followed seemed to become a part of everyone's face.

The operations officer, Asher, unrolled the map. We were in Shivta, an archaeological site, facing the remains of the desert city of the Nabatteans. Surrounding the headquarters were our unit's tents. We were responsible at that point for the section of the Egyptian frontier from Gabel Keren in the north to Wadi Lotz in the south. This was an area of hills and dunes, surrounding and safeguarding the Abu-Ageila–Nitzama–Beer-Sheba road, a road which our Intelligence had informed us was to be used as a central approach line by the Egyptian forces for entrance into the Negev. "By advancing along this road," Asher said, "they will be in a position to isolate the lower Negev and join with the Jordanian forces from the Mount Hebron area." Large square letters were drawn in black pencil on the map: Phase A *Defense*. The border was marked in green, straight and definite, with a multitude of blue and red marks to indicate the different units. Behind these marks were people. Under cover of code numbers hid vehicles and arms. The tip of the stick, now drawing imaginary lines, suggested the enormous machine, motivated by the undebatable need to survive, which had been mobilized a few days earlier and was now being held there between the green line and our yellow reality, ready to meet a threat or to present one.

"Why talk so much?" Asher said. "Let's go and see them." It was midday. The sun in its zenith was drying the few scattered gray desert shrubs, drying the skin, drying the drops of sweat, enervating the will power. I changed my sandals for boots and got myself a water bottle and an army writing pad. My official assignment was "correspondent for the military spokesman," which meant that I would be attached to the division throughout the period of mobilization. I was to send to the correspondents' pool daily reports which were to be distributed for publication in the various newspapers in Israel and abroad. For the time being this was my work, but there was no question in my mind that in case of war I would be first a soldier, an officer, able and willing to fulfill other duties. Equipped with a wide-brimmed khaki hat, I joined Asher on the jeep and we were on our way.

How long it takes us to gather the component parts of our memory—the problems, self-appraisals, the self-analysis, our little daily dilemmas, petty quests for comfort. And how quickly they all can disappear. We were driving fast along the road heading west, toward the green line on the map, and with each mile I shed another layer. Not a process of pensive days and dream-filled nights but a short jeep drive, the hair already uncombable, face burning, muscles adjusting to the hard seat and the bumpy road, hat fighting the wind, sunglasses fighting the reflected glare from the dunes. Between Shivta and the armored brigade camp, London was dumped; Paris was lost from there to Ktziot; Pucci and Trigère were forgotten with the first grease marks on my khaki trousers, my car with the sight of heavy bulldozers blocking the road, while Rome and Athens disappeared among the rocky hills of Nitzana as we approached Beerotaim, headquarters of the battalion which was "sitting on the border."

Beerotaim, situated on the summit of a hill, is a spot of green grass and a few wooden huts. All that was behind, stretching east—the dunes, the craters, the Dead Sea, and the valley halved by the Jordanian frontier—was ours. All that was ahead and west—more dunes, chalk hills, the Sinai Desert to the Canal—was theirs; here, near Beerotaim, the asphalt road ended for us like an exclamation mark crossing the border to the other side. We were offered lunch in the battalion's dining room, cooked food, in spite of it being Saturday, by special permission of the chief rabbi. The battalion commander took me to see his men. And one needed a guide to discern them. Never before had Israeli units been so well fortified, entrenched, camouflaged, and hidden; the terrain, untouched for thousands of years, had opened thousands of jaws to engulf and hide a whole division. Tanks, artillery, supply trucks, busses, ambulances, soldiers, were all dug in and covered; only antennae here and there betrayed a headquarters, and clouds of moving dust suggested the movements of vehicles. The hills, usually of eternal purity, looked slightly scarred where white spots of fresh loess indicated recent digging. Under the overhead shelters, in the bunkers and the trenches, was our army: facing east, tuned in to the radio, in a state of readiness, and wondering what the next moment might bring.

"Someone said it would take bulldozers to pull them out of the trenches now," the commander commented. We climbed into another jeep and rode to "Little Sabcha," our foremost defense position in the area. To meet the soldiers we had to walk from trench to trench. They were all reservists. Men in their thirties mostly, all family men. The usual exchange of smiles, the banal questions: Where are you from? Ashdod (a new port town populated mostly by new immigrants). What do you do as a civilian? I am a plumber. Children? Four. How many years in Israel? Five. Origin? North Africa. How long have you been here? One week. Was drafted last Friday, had no time to take anything. Not worried about the family, we write postcards. It was hard work, but now we are just waiting. Name? Karta, Sammy, Cohen, Sebag, Raziel. Plumbers, clerks, farmers, porters, a shoemaker, a tailor, a bank manager. North Africa, Yemen, Hungary, Poland, Tel-Aviv. Three children and supporting old parents. Widower, five children—two in the army. Dark with curly sideburns, blue-eyed and blond, a redhead, a bearded Yemenite, pink skinned

4

and badly sunburned. French accent, Arab words mixed with Hebrew, central European pronunciation, Sabra slang. Saturday afternoon in the "Little Sabcha."

This was my first encounter with the soldiers. They all wanted an answer to What will happen? They joked and humored me, a few prayed at sunset, some wrote cards home. Through my binoculars I could see the enemy. A group of Egyptian soldiers were silhouetted on the "Big Sabcha" facing us. They, too, were well fortified. They were watching us. Their barrels reflected the setting sun and they, too, were waiting. Between the two "Sabchas" rested the desert, a road, cracked soil hiding mines and the repeated question: What will happen next?

"Are they good soldiers?" I asked Bari, the commander.

"Some are. They will make an unbeatable defense line; as for attack, they have never been tested. I suppose I can count on 40 per cent. For the rest, I wouldn't like to say."

I left them with a sense of pride rather than security. Do they love this stretch of desert the way we were brought up to? And how brave would they prove to be compared with the fewer regulars?

When darkness took over, war seemed remote. The desert died its nightly death; there were no lights to be seen. There would be ambushes and a few patrols to make sure the green line was not crossed; an occasional breeze brought with it a song sung by a waiting soldier. The songs and the words, the maps and the plans implied few worries perhaps, but there was great tension, and with nightfall came the sadness of the isolated and the loneliness of the exposed. Shivta, on our return, meant home now—the familiar dark tents, the endless chatter of the radio sets. Rachamim the cook was brewing hot tea for the general and there was the comforting silhouette of his trailer, always open, always inviting. General Sharon invited me in for a briefing. I was suspicious of Arik Sharon in the way I am suspicious of all men who have become legends in their own lives, including my father. Having won my battle

5

the day before, when my demand to go south was finally granted, I had suggested I join Arik's headquarters. I had been motivated by a desire to verify or disprove to myself the qualities attributed to him. When I climbed the ladder to the trailer, he met me with a charming smile and stood up to shake my hand and introduce to me two officers attending him. A handsome face, smiling eyes, straight nose, a body perhaps too heavy but comfortably so in battle uniform, dark khakis. There was a paratrooper's red beret within hand's reach. In spite of his looks and comparative youth, his hair was silvery, wavy, hiding a high forehead.

The trailer, which was later to become a symbol when it reappeared after four days in battle in the middle of the Sinai, was as impersonal and as simple as possible. Two wooden benches were used as beds at night. There was a large table which was used in turns for eating and working, a small cupboard stuffed with papers and small supplies, a water container with a tap, soap, mirror, and towel. Arik's personal belongings fitted into a rucksack smaller than mine, and three blankets were folded under a windbreaker. "I am glad you are with us," he said, and added that I should feel free to ask for whatever help or information I might need. I asked him if there was anything he would like me to concentrate on during the days to come, and he suggested that I visit the auxiliary forces, usually little mentioned and deserving much—the engineers' battalion which did the bulk of the fortification job, the supply service battalion, whose job was to make the long wait as comfortable as possible, and the field hospital. We talked of other things. He wanted to know about the fighting in Vietnam which I had covered a couple of months earlier, about the Far East in general, and, reflecting the obsession of his own thoughts rather than seeking an answer: Are we on the eve of war? We all wished we had the answer, we all feared the answer, but the uncertainty was worse.

I had a sleeping bag and was given the front seat of a station wagon as my first night's accommodation. The alternative, which I chose the following night, was a trench in the sand. Being rather small, I curled up and stuck my feet out of the window. Trying to ignore the desert chill and the snores of the sleeper in the back seat, I fell asleep.

I awoke at four. The light was already strong but mercifully the heat had not yet returned. The camp's morning commotion was like a memory of eleven years back pushing its way to the surface. Sleepy faces peeping out of sleeping bags hoping to discover it was still night, the shaking and folding of blankets, stretching of arms, a platoon marching toward the road, a log fire heating water in a kettle, men shaving in cars' side mirrors. I put on my boots—the only item I had taken off for the night—and washed my face and teeth in my canteen water—deliciously cool now. A square canvas structure marked "girl soldiers" served as lavatory. Breakfast comprised a hard-boiled egg, bread, a tomato, and sweet, tepid tea. I gave up combing my hair and decided to braid it. The dust that clung hopelessly to skin and clothes did not really feel like dirt, but I envied the men who were enjoying field showers along the road, waving to one another, naked or wrapped in towels, a strange sight in the middle of nowhere.

Again in the jeep, again westward. On my way to the infantry brigade headquarters I stopped at the engineers' battalion. Near one of the tents several soldiers were grouped around a guitar player; high up on their machines, listening to the songs, were the bulldozer operators. The bulldozers were huge and yellow, loved and pampered by the operators—"My D-8," "Super 8," "D-9," "D-4"—and nicknamed after women. . . . The operators' eyes were red, a result of days and nights of work. "We have changed the view here," they said, "then changed it back to normal." They had opened a new road heading south, enabling the fortifications to be built quickly. "And if it happens?" A small group gathered round us. "We'll

7

open roads, clear minefields, push with our forces." The guitarist was singing 'She Loves Me" and a D-8 was digging a trench for itself. "No time for archaeology," Amiram said. In the past he would call my father whenever he unearthed something which may have been a tomb or an ancient dwelling. "What part of the fortification is of permanent value?" "Only the trenches in the hills. They were a tough piece of work, but they will last forever. The work in the dunes will be gone with the desert winds in a few weeks, but by then who knows where we'll be?"

They showed me pictures of their children, a postcard from some school children, and offered me a piece of home-made cake. They asked, knowing I didn't have an answer, how long I thought it would last? Not nervously, not even hopefully, but in a dry, disguised tone. "See you back in Tel-Aviv," I said. "Or in Cairo," they said.

Approaching the infantry brigade war room, I saw a familiar face. Blond hair made lighter by the dust, laughing blue eyes, tanned face. 1 recognized the Tel-Aviv artist I had often met in a Diessengoff café—Hovav. "Have you heard the news?" he asked. My heart stopped beating. It's happened, I thought. "Five prisoners! On the hill across the road. They just appeared in a jeep, must have lost their way."

They had been taken away when I arrived, but the soldiers who had captured them told their story. Three were officers, one a lieutenant colonel. They had driven almost into the fortified area and had been shocked to find themselves surrounded by Israelis. Our soldiers were as amazed, and a moment of indecision followed. Then they were searched and blindfolded, and driven away to the brigade headquarters, where their vehicle, a Russian jeep, was left. The officers were carrying guns, the two soldiers were drivers. "If you don't react they won't harm you," our soldiers heard the lieutenant colonel say. Our own men were bewildered by two facts: The lack of basic knowledge of the area which had enabled enemy officers to make such a stupid mistake as to follow the road

8

once it crossed the border and to drive straight into the trenches offering no resistance. Also, as Uri put it, "You should have seen the difference between the officers and the soldiers. The officers were clean, well groomed, their clothes made of a type of silk"—though here perhaps his imagination was running away with him—"clean handkerchiefs which they offered us when we blindfolded them, so polite and soft. The soldiers looked unshaven, dirty, wearing rags, scared to death."

"They haven't changed," murmured an officer who had fought in the Sinai Campaign. "The same army, in spite of all this talk of changes and progress."

"Their fingernails were manicured and they smelt of cologne," someone else commented.

Perhaps these young fellows were wrong to refuse to associate cologne with the image of an officer, but they did know that General Arik Sharon and his driver Yoram wore the same battle dress and the same quality boots. They knew also that the infantry brigade commander and the gunner ate the same C-rations in the field, and usually they addressed their officer by his first name. It was with contempt rather than hatred that these young men—they were regular soldiers—spoke about this first encounter with the enemy.

It also made the enemy's proximity very real. Suddenly they were people who could make a mistake of a few hundred yards and be in the middle of us; by the same token we could be among them just as fast, as a result of an order. We drove to Beer-Sheba to file the story. Staying there even for a few hours proved unbearable. The city was crowded with soldiers, army cars, journalists. Instead of the silence of the desert, the nerve-racking wait, there was the interminable political chatter. It was with a tremendous sense of relief that I turned to go back that night. On the way we heard Prime Minister Eshkol's speech to the nation. Other than "embarrassing" I find it difficult to describe. Slow, uncertain, noncommittal, uninspiring, it gave the listeners anything but an answer, even a

9

provisional one, even the courage to continue the wait. I thought of the men in the trenches, listening to the speech —the first official statement in days—while trying to pierce through the darkness around them to spot any movement. Listening to those words, away from home, how could they feel secure, how could they feel that their homes were secure? I believe that this speech was a turning point. From then on the people took over, and pressure of public opinion—although of what range and to what effect we shall never know—to form a wall-to-wall government began to mount.

After hearing the speech and leaving the desert capital behind, arriving in Shivta had a new meaning. We were instructed to drive with dimmed lights. It was late and cold and the darkness was most welcome. I fumbled for my sleeping bag and cuddled to the inner wall of the shallow trench. The North Star shone above Beer-Sheba, Tel-Aviv, over Paris and London; the sand felt humid. Whatever the political leadership, I knew that the army was strong in itself; and here, in its lap, I felt a security that, paradoxically, did not leave me until I had returned home. A feeling of safety in action, the closeness of people certain of victory because of their ability, professionalism, and true spirit. I fell asleep. Someone shook me. "Turgeman, your time to watch."

"I am not Turgeman," I said. Perhaps I was in the wrong trench.

Monday morning found us with new instructions. We no longer believed that it was a matter of "any moment now."

Arik issued new instructions. The spontaneous, rather casual behavior and appearance of the troops were to disappear, to be replaced by an established military routine. Next to the check post, small tents were erected in which the barbers cut the soldiers' hair. Shaving was compulsory, and walking around without weapon or helmet resulted in punishment. Prisons were built and M.P. platoons arrived from Beer-Sheba. Training was to resume in all units. The new orders were executed immediately. Whether looking for an answer in the face of a commander, searching the roads, or scanning the sky whenever an aircraft droned above us, in the eyes of the soldiers a new expression of stubborn responsibility was growing. The key words now were "patience" and "a deep breath," and for some reason we all talked about "a two weeks' wait." The immediate task now had to do with ability to last out in this no-man's land of time—a problem also for the economy of the country now evacuated of its manpower, for the families of the soldiers and reservists, but most of all for the men themselves, who had to be in a state of readiness while adjusting to a new routine, to long marches, and the growing sense of separation from home.

The sand and the dust now stopped being an overnight hardship and became permanent phenomena; our helmet and our rifle new natural limbs. An army of reservists was to be transformed into a body of regulars, united, trained, patient. The first doubts were beginning to be heard. "We are used to fast action, we shall not be able to survive like this for long," "the high morale will not last the week," "the economy will collapse," and the like. On Tuesday afternoon I drove to some units to see if the change had affected them.

It was a sad day. Somehow the army began this toughest week of all. The tension was slackening and the men began to look around and wonder, to ask questions, and sense the heat, the average cooking, the flies during the day and the mosquitoes at night. They had been ready to go, and now they were beginning to think.

Many of the reservists could speak Arabic. Occasionally they tuned in to Radio Cairo, and what they heard was far from the cautious tone of their own prime minister. Colonel Nasser was inviting them to meet a failure; he bragged and boasted and fanned the hatred of his troops. "If we aren't going to move, why do they keep us here?" I was asked on Tuesday. The general feeling was disappointment. That same day Nasser had declared, "If we have succeeded in restoring the situation to what it was before 1956 there is no doubt that we shall restore the situation to what it was prior to 1948."

"So what are we waiting for?" I was asked, and I found myself asking the same question.

By that afternoon all the soldiers had shaved and had their hair cut. Where before there had been fortification work, now platoons were seen marching and singing and the Nitzana area looked like a huge camp in its daily training routine. Training was not done just for the sake of keeping the army busy. A variety of possibilities was properly analyzed and the training involved executing some of the details. Coordination between army and infantry, physical adjustment to the dunes area, communications systems, methods of attack—all these were rehearsed and repeated, each hour of training being an added security, developing the ability of the soldiers to perform in the method and manner that would be demanded of them when or if the time came. In the afternoon I arrived in the "Little Sabcha." It was three in the afternoon, and there was no shade at all. The soldiers were sitting on top of the chalk-stone hill and a group of singers was performing for them. An accordionist, a guitarist, and the singers Miri, Zipi, and Aliza. They looked ill-kept, they had been performing several times a day and sleeping a few hours each night, but what they gave the soldiers was irreplaceable. The Egyptians watching must have been surprised. The men were applauding in rhythm, here, at the end of the road, on the green line. The first song was the Sinai Campaign 1956 hit "Confronting Mount Sinai"; they followed with Palmach 1948 songs, songs in Yiddish, in Polish, and in Arabic. The performers were not brilliant but at that moment they were the soldiers' national theater, Philharmonic orchestra, and opera house combined. After they had left, a soft afternoon breeze touched the Sabcha outpost. The men returned to their trenches, giving me a few postcards to post for them. "You can read them, if you like," they said, proudly showing me drawings they had received from their children. Most of the cards attempted to calm the families left behind, all saying, "I'll soon be back, after the Victory." Postcards in Hungarian, in Arabic, in French, in Hebrew, and in Rumanian. These men had been there for ten days now, twice they had been packed and ready to march, and they worked day and night.

Returning to headquarters, I asked an officer friend to take me to the ancient city of Shivta. We mounted the jeep and drove along our own marked minefields to the yellow walls of the Nabattean town. The sun was setting and the half-preserved dome of a Byzantine church reflected its last rays. Should I kneel down in prayer? But what would I pray for? I think it was this moment that brought to me the realization that I wanted war, but I had no right to admit it. Not war for the excitement of it, not even war for victory's sake, but war as a solution to a situation that was unbearable. Not war to kill, but war in order not to be killed. Shivta, empty of tourists, was beautiful, clothed in gold, covered with dust. No footprints, but stones to tell the endless story of conquests and desertions. We walked along the two-thousand-year-old streets of the town. Caravans had stopped here on their way from Petra to Gaza. From a short distance I could see the tents of our field hospital. My officer friend and I talked for about an hour. I was holding back unwanted tears. I, too, must have gone through this change of morale. I, too, was looking for an answer of sorts. The straits of Tiran were closed. Sinai was heavy with seven infantry divisions and two armored divisions and what was going to happen to us? Anything seemed better than just waiting for it to happen and when people said, "It is going to be a long and bad war," I thought I knew what they meant. I had a desperate feeling, as if awaiting some signal, some kind of green light. I felt alone.

Back in camp that evening, a pile of letters and cables awaited me, mostly from friends abroad. They cared, they identified, they encouraged, but they were worried. They offered help, but sometimes it was like the last cigarette offered to the doomed man. Someone offered me a ticket abroad and a house in Italy; they all begged to take care. I missed a few of my friends but I could not really write and tell them about it. Tell them what? One would have to start with David and Solomon, the temples, the exiles. One would have to retell of concentration camps and war horrors, of 1948 and 1949 and every week that followed. A letter answering to "How are you?" would mean reciting the Bible, the Talmud, Alterman's poetry, singing Hefer's songs, describing the 1956 campaign, and telling of Nasser's broadcasts. All these things made me what I was and nothing else mattered. So I didn't write, and hoped they would understand that their support meant a great deal. "So there will not be a war," one of the drivers said to me. "So there will be a war," I snapped back. It was a warm night and I slept outside again after a long walk.

The following morning, Wednesday the thirtieth, brought a new situation. King Hussein had signed a defense agreement with Nasser and announced that "the hour of decision has arrived." Parcels arrived that morning and were distributed to the girl soldiers—white framed sunglasses, wash 'n' dry tissues, chap sticks, and cologne. If "the hour of decision had arrived" we did not know of it. Other correspondents returned to Beer-Sheba or Tel-Aviv; there was nothing new to write about. Leaves for twenty-four hours were granted to 10 per cent of the troops and people began wondering what life was like "back home." "Back home," meanwhile, knew a wave of devotion and dedication. Everybody volunteered to do something, money was donated, people were gentler, kinder, more polite. They gave of their time and means, the country was a living room populated by one large family. Schools sent youngsters to help kibbutzim in farm work, and Boy Scouts distributed the mail and the milk as the men watched the frontiers. Exhilarating news of the public opinion and mood in various countries reached us, and in Israel's embassies throughout the world volunteers queued to be listed and drafted. We were the underdog going through our finest hour.

A couple of provocative acts by the Egyptians were met with silence. We received cream cakes from the Welfare Committee for Soldiers. Elderly men exempted from the draft came crying, begging to be employed; women and children dug trenches and filled sacks with sand; on the radio news broadcasts alternated with sentimental songs, and Syria and Jordan and Egypt were on the borders backed by the armies of Iraq, Algeria, Kuwait, Lebanon, and Sudan. I asked to join a reconnaissance patrol heading south along the Sinai border. The patrol was composed of two command cars—about two platoons of reservists, two officers. The purpose of the patrol was to make sure that the track had not been mined, so the first command car moved forward slowly, taking the risk, searching for signs, and the second followed in its tracks. We would arrive at the outpost facing Kadesh Barnea where the children of Israel had camped when they left Egypt and where now, with a good pair of binoculars, a large concentration of arms could be seen.

I was sitting on, or rather holding on to, the wooden frame, trying to avoid the bumps. Next to me was Private Shimon Albaz. He was holding an F.N. machine gun and I held on to my UZI, an Israeli submachine gun. We talked French. Albaz speaks funny Hebrew. He has been in the country three years, works as a porter in Ashdod, is married, has three children. He pulled from his wallet a photo—all the men did that when I asked them whether they had children. It was his first patrol. He looked around, tense and ready to jump.

"The minute I see them I'll shoot and hit," he declared.

"But we are within Israel's territory," I said.

"Where is the border?" he asked.

We were in a wadi now, and climbing up, I showed him the border stone.

"And all that over there is theirs?"

"Yes."

We stopped at some Nabbatean wells. The commander sent a few soldiers to safeguard the area and explained to the others the ancient system of gathering water. He was a teacher now, and I watched Albaz listen. He asked, "Why don't we have agriculture here now?" A gazelle crossed our path, swift and elegant, and the beauty of its climb up the cliffs was breathtaking. I asked Albaz if he loved the Negev. "It is ours, so I love it," was his answer. Other soldiers nodded. I felt the gap then. I loved it for its wild beauty, in the way that I loved the Sinai, which was not yet ours. I loved the space and the chill at night and the starry, clear desert sky. I loved the canyons and the surprises behind wadi turns, the craters, and the enormity and eternity of it all. I loved it for itself, uncultivated, untouched, pure and exposed, while the soldiers were wonderfully possessive about it. No, a Budapest man said, it was not beautiful, he missed the green.

We arrived at the top of the hill. A plateau stretched before us. Kseime. Tanks, outposts, a camp, movement of armor on the road, the reality of the enemy. Albaz aimed his gun. "Too far!" he declared naïvely. I was thinking about shots that triggered off wars. Did it really matter who fired the first shot? Did it matter what councils and governments decided? Too much was at stake for us—everything. If being the first to shoot gained us an advantage, let us be condemned for it; life here mattered more than some petty formality. We were offered lemonade, given—as usual—postcards to mail, among which was one to the school children of Dimona thanking them for their greetings to this particular infantry unit and telling them not to worry. Leaving them behind, I felt guilt. I was free to move, I stayed in Shivta out of choice, and I isolated myself because it suited me, because I felt I belonged where I was. They had to be there, waiting for their water supply and depending on the radio and the communication system. They were perched on the summit of the hill like a flag, aware of the gathering of forces in front of them. We became for them another cloud of dust as we descended in first gear to the wadi and northward.

That evening I had to go to Beer-Sheba to deliver some articles. The neon lights of the city disturbed me deeply. I went with a friend to the officers' club. It was empty. I asked the waitress what day of the week it was, and she smiled and put her hand on my shoulder. "You'd be surprised," she said, "how many people ask the same question." The luxuries of a city— hot showers, large mirrors, ice cream. A meal which was different, a child's cry, civilian cars. Beer-Sheba, as in the Sinai Campaign, took on the role of capital. It offered thousands of soldiers their last glimpse of civilization when they left for the south and the first when they came back home. I called Shivta to apologize for not returning, although this was unnecessary, and spent a sleepless night on a tough bed.

On Wednesday I returned to Shivta and decided there and then that unless something very extraordinary happened I was not leaving the place. The half tent erected for correspondents was pulled down as the others left. I felt I was part of the unit now, not an observer able to come and go. I moved my belongings into a large tent which I shared with two officers, and it was then that I realized the range and quality of activity that went on.

If during the first few days I had concentrated on learning what our men were like, now I wanted to know what we were facing, why we were there, and what our plans were— just in case . . . Oddly, I felt like a spy. I was not present at the different planning meetings which took place nightly. I did not enter the war room or did I have access to the Intelligence reports, but I sat there watching and listening. Faces of people, worried, tense, excited, disappointed. Changes on the map, arrival of brigade commanders and general headquarters coordinating officers, occasionally a few words of explanation from Arik. The 2nd Division facing us had two strongholds— Abu-Ageila and Kseime, both acting as blockades on major Sinai roads leading west and north. In addition they held several outposts which we could see. The fact that they outnumbered us, in armor, artillery, and number of soldiers, never worried me, although numbers quoted were impressive. I was fascinated by pieces of reports which reached us hourly and by our fast reaction to them, giving the enemy credit for knowing our organization thoroughly, giving it maximum credit for planning and changing our plans accordingly. In town, people demanded more people in the government and in the field the soldiers waited for war, but here in division headquarters it seemed as though war was being waged. The soldiers in the trench had to wait, the officers in the war room were working day and night. The enemy have moved another hundred tanks! They have moved another fifty! Another battalion has arrived! Our Intelligence service was continually feeding the war room—air photographs, radio reports, changes of positions, detailed information from our own outposts. From the outside it seemed like a game. A helicopter landing: the maps are pulled out, the arrows in red and blue and black erased and new ones painted; orders are given to the units; commanders arrive in the middle of the night; every step is weighed and replanned over and over in an effort to tease out the best solution.

In the Sinai campaign we exploited to the full the element of surprise. Here it had to be the surprise of brilliance based on knowledge of enemy methods—to hit what was least expected, from an unexpected direction in an unexpected way. Colonel Dov, regularly a faculty member of the National Defense College and now one of Arik's right-hand men, explained it to me. They have a system, not a bad one, but bound by conventions. They have forces and they move them according to the books. We know the books, we have done the exercises, and our advantage lies in forgetting them all and finding the one method which is not in the books. But then, neither were these men from any written book. Dov moved around wearing a girl friend's corduroy hat; Arik had with him a couple of friends, one a civilian ranch owner, the other Zeevale, a drafted captain from Nahalal, the farm I grew up on. The amored brigade commander, Motke, had the appearance of a teacher, and Kuti, the infantry brigade commander, rather fierce looking and famous for his courage, daring, and leadership, was dreaming of having a cattle farm in the mountains, and told me he would never kill. David, Arik's A.D.C., insisted on analyzing poetry with me, and I suspect that he wrote poetry himself. In the afternoon I went to the armored brigade to talk to Motke. I had to decide where I should be in case of war. Motke, bespectacled, curly-haired, was barefoot. His small trailer was operational rather than comfortable. A desk, a bed, a couple of chairs with hardly any room between them. I accepted a glass of brandy and some biscuits and listened to Motke. He quoted poetry and recited some lines from the Bible to support his argument. Motke was a teacher, he knew where our strength lay and issued daily bulletins to the soldiers, encouraging and preparing them. He looked harmless enough sitting there, but I knew that here was a lion, proud, convinced, eager. He offered me room in his half-track, "a lift to the battle front," and I duly accepted. I was planning on going with the brigade, as long as I didn't have to be closed up inside a tank. But at that point, five days before the war, talking about "where to be" seemed like wishful thinking.

A patrol was leaving for Beerotaim that evening in order to set off from there at dawn to explore the frontier. I decided to go with them, as after sunset individual traffic was forbidden. Darkness engulfed us while we were on our way. The driver of a jeep gave me a flight jacket and we drove along the road without lights. Something about this drive broke the monotony of waiting. Very few lights could be noticed in the area. Some antiaircraft guns and antennae were like warning fingers, silhouetted against the Negev sky, and a strong, cool wind blew in our faces. The machine gun attached to the jeep was loaded and the cartridges reflected the light of a pale moon. We drove in silence. Around us was the empty and uninhabited land, except for the troops which were dug in. There were no smells, no sounds, no colors, the emptiness of an area which nevertheless was all we had and which needed protection. I thought of the soldiers in the north, where every patrol route was surrounded by orchards and fields, where there were children and women, barking dogs, sleeping flocks. There it was clear what had to be protected and defended; here it was only wilderness, but wilderness which we had learned to love rather than fear and which we would hold on to as if it were a living city with streets and lives and a future.

We arrived in Beerotaim after eleven and I joined a group of soldiers in a camouflaged bunker. They were making Turkish coffee on a small log fire and singing quietly. They wanted to talk. They were reservists. What constituted morale? was the question we tried to answer. The first week it had been obvious. Old 1948 and 1956 songs on the radio, cream cakes from home, letters from school children. Morale was built up by extreme danger, by the cheering talk of unit commanders, by a sense of unity of troops ready to march. Now it was different. All those elements now seemed like a substitute for the "real thing." Entertainers could not dissolve the sight of an enemy tank and little parcels from back home could not open the road leading west.

We were asked to be patient, they said, but we want more information—one good explanation of what is happening will be sufficient to keep us going for weeks. For an hour we tried to analyze the situation. Was Nasser really sure of his victory? Did he really want war or was he simply committed to his previous boastful statements so that now he had no way out? They seemed to grasp the notion that diplomacy should be given a chance before the armor took over and also to realize that time was not being lost or wasted by waiting but that a right public mood was being built for whatever might happen and that a stronger and better-trained army was being formed. "It is talks like this one that build up morale," one of them said as I was leaving. "We have to understand in order to act or to refrain from action. We are not automatons. There lies one difference between us and the other side." They had three hours to sleep before morning patrol. I found an empty truck where I lay awake on a mattress made of a camouflage net.

Some Druze soldiers stationed in Beerotaim made hot coffee in the morning and I left for the infantry brigade headquarters to join the brigade commander.

He set off for one of our outposts. Kuti, the brigade commander, is a black-haired, dark-skinned mustached colonel. Dressed in dark khaki and a beret, equipped with a pistol, water canteen, a knife, and binoculars, he looks like a warrior. His soft voice, the smile in his eyes, his speech, suggest the contrary. "The area is full of arrowheads," he said, looking for a good spot from which to watch the border patrol. At times he bent down to pick up a flint stone and dismissed it as useless. "Tomorrow," he told me, "report early and we'll go looking for arrowheads. I know a place which must have been a workshop thousands of years ago. I gave your father some." Kuti didn't know archaeology well, but he certainly sensed and smelled it, and I accepted the offered date. He sat on a large stone and watched the horizon for the first half-tracks to appear. "I want us on the frontier," I had heard Arik say the night before. "From border stone to border stone, not even parallel, but on the last inch which is Israel." Was the purpose to warm up the border? I asked. No, just a test, an establishment of facts to make sure there were no mines, to create some activity to show we were not dormant. The sun was merciless. Kuti offered me some chocolate. "You should always carry chocolate and biscuits," he said. A cloud of dust on the horizon announced our half-tracks. With my binoculars I could see them clearly. They paused near a border stone that touched the U.N. patrol road and continued, followed by a few jeeps. Working their way slowly in the deep dunes, they approached us; we moved back and watched them printing the green line on the map in khaki and metal. In the air hovered frustration. We seemed to be playing games. We watched the enemy watch us and wished they would move.

By lunchtime the patrol had covered the frontier in our area and returned to headquarters. We wondered if they would think the patrol was to be a daily event and if they would try to lay mines. I returned to Shivta.

In the afternoon I went with Colonel Dov to visit the field hospital. A few tents were fighting the afternoon sandstorm and ambulances surrounded the unit area. Two senior doctors in shorts offered me coffee; the place had the deserted comfort of an unemployed unit. The doctors held important positions in civilian hospitals and were heads of surgical units. "We can operate on four tables simultaneously in the field." We walked through the empty tents. Dov walked away with a female lieutenant to enjoy some cool soft drinks—a luxury that only hospitals or quartermasters seemed to be able to afford. Large boxes offered sterility to instruments, sheets, bottles—all disposable. A small Frigidaire held a supply of blood, plasma, and infusion liquids; the metal operating tables looked primitive and lonely. "We can move in two units, independently. Each unit has two operation crews and a good number of doctors. We will operate on cases which cannot be evacuated to the rear and treat the wounded so that they will reach the hospitals after the first medical aid has been given them." "What are you engaged in now?" I asked. "Our doctors give lectures to the first-aid men and the medics, on a variety of cases. The few sick we have refuse to be hospitalized and demand to go back to the units. We attend all the headquarters meetings, every change in plans affects us. We have to know whether the hospital will be on the road or static, we have to calculate the possible number of casualties and the type. This we can do if we know the kind of war we are facing, artillery or mines, infantry battles or air attacks." There, in Shivta, in the evening, war seemed remote. Dr. Agmon talked of mines, but the ambulances seemed rooted to the ground and the night seemed safe. Perhaps those boxes, with all their instruments inside, would never be opened, the blood supply never used. I could not help hoping that these

22

people would remain unemployed, but I knew that if war were to come there could be no better team. They were wearing uniforms. "Yes, we have all we need. Electricity, infusion instruments, blood, and special training." "Will you give priority to an enemy wounded if his case is more urgent than one of ours?" "I think I will. It is bound to happen, it has happened before; but it is difficult to answer beforehand."

Dov came back with Dr. Mordehai who was in charge of the surgical team. The doctor was explaining and complaining that with a couple of million Israeli pounds the army could have been fitted out with the most modern surgeries and operating theaters. He was not sure he would be able to complete an operation without getting covered with dust. Dov listened skeptically. "You'll never use your fine instruments," he said to the doctor. "Last time, in '56, my brother the surgeon was with us at Mitla Pass. We had quite a number of wounded there that day, but all were quickly evacuated to Beer-Sheba or Tel Hashomer, and this saved them. My brother thought that a delay of an hour or two would be less dangerous than operating under field conditions—and you never have enough doctors or space or time in the battle. I bet you anything, Doctor, that all the serious cases will be evacuated by helicopters."

On the way back in the jeep Dov added and elaborated in the vein of an instructor at the Defense College: "You have always to fall back to the question where to invest your money, what system of weapons or organization will give you the maximum security or returns. There are always more needs and demands from the services of the army, air force, and navy than the money and resources available and at your disposal. It's a problem of economics of defense." It was wise ... the "civilian" medical base—on the hospitals in the ... helicopters which could be used for quick ...ded and for many other purposes such as ...its in the rear of the enemy positions or ...reconnaissance. "But you're not listening," he complained as he finished his lecture. True, I was thinking of those wounded and needing help on the spot and not about more economical systems.

Back in Shivta there was talk about the different offers my father had received—"military adviser," "a high position in the army," and the like. We had dinner and listened to the news broadcast at eleven. Negotiations were on, and my father was refusing to accept a fictitious position which gave him no authority. He was either going to take responsibility or stay with the troops, in whatever capacity; he was not going to be a front whose only purpose was to satisfy a mounting demand for a larger cabinet and the inclusion of military professionals in our leadership. I did not wait for the midnight news in which his appointment was announced. I fell asleep as soon a my head touched the pillow.

On Friday morning I was told that my father had been appointed Minister of Defense. Even though I tried hard to be objective I could not help noticing that the appointment had caused an immediate change, quite noticeable and positive, wherever one looked. Commanders and soldiers alike seemed to have been given a second wind, they knew now that even the wait made sense. Although there was no real justification in associating General Dayan with a decision to start the war (which we claimed had been declared by the sea blockade in the Gulf of Eilat), somehow we felt that we were all there for a purpose and that there would soon be a move. A few weeks prior to his appointment he had visited Arik's war room and had expressed his esteem and approval. The plans, he thought, were excellent, detailed, brilliant, and operational. Arik mentioned it to me during my stay, and now with the appointment we knew that there would be no change in our plans. I felt, on top of my personal pride, a new sense curity. Remembering the hesitant speech of th ister and the noncommittal though brilli nouncement of our foreign minister, knowing that my father was a man of commanders read the maps in a new way—the symbols were now well-known reality.

Saturday in the desert is not marked by anything. In the town traffic dies down and the shops are closed, children wear their best clothes, and the beaches are crowded. For us it was just another day. The chief rabbi of the army had arrived the night before to spend the weekend with our armored division. He was not preaching war but victory, distributing prayer books and Bibles and a printed one-page prayer for soldiers—pocket size. We had a long breakfast in the trailer. Arik had an unlimited capacity for food. The Intelligence officer arrived to announce a change in enemy forces. They had moved a tank battalion south along the border and Arik gave instructions to send a few tanks on a patrol along our side of the border to face them and block the wadi entrance which they may be planning to use. This was routine. Every move during those days was followed immediately by a countermove of our forces, at times real and sometimes fake—for instance, vehicles were moved in circles to create an illusion of large numbers on the move. Colonel Uri was given the Bell helicopter to supervise the patrol and the pilot agreed that I was light enough to join the ride in the two-seater. We flew very low above our lines—an armored brigade composed of three battalions; one Centurion battalion commanded by Natke; the others, Sherman tanks and armored infantry, headed by Sason and Herzel; a specially combined reconnaissance force with AMX light tanks and half-tracks and jeeps commanded by Arie. We flew over the infantry brigade—two regular battalions and one of reservists—Ofer, laughter in his eyes; Dov, bearded; and Castel, boasting a large black mustache, commanded them. Our artillery was composed of six battalions: short, medium, and long-barreled and well dispersed and dug in, commanded by the blue-eyed, dark-haired Yaakov.

Close along the border, well dug in, was a specially combined force commanded by Colonel Uri, mainly for defense but able in case of need to move forward toward Kseime. The cliffs along the border are high and imposing. The little helicopter looked like a flea hopping from peak to peak, stopping occasionally at outposts and following the track along which the few tanks and jeeps moved south. Uri made sure the first jeeps had arrived at the wadi entrance from which we could see the new enemy concentration of armor. We were offered a meal and coffee. Later we had to walk up a hill for the helicopter to take off. The heat had affected the Bell and limited its take-off power. On our return journey I could not help feeling that there was something pathetic about our defense system. In some of the outposts there were only five or ten soldiers. We were scattered along a long frontier and we tried to give the impression of a much larger force. For some reason I thought of the fund-raising tours I had made in recent years. Very often when I talked of defense problems my listeners would nod; they treated it now as a sort of gimmick, almost a trick. Whenever I talked about the "few against many," people would say, "We know, we know." But here it all was—Mount Chorsha, twenty people, Mount Sagi, wadi Los, Mount Meara, the low tents, a communication set, a few boxes of K-rations, and a water container. Not a tree in sight, the occasional visit to look forward to, the transistor radio broadcasting news, advertisements or pop songs, a gazelle or desert mouse, loneliness. Uri left us in his headquarters and I returned with the helicopter back to Shivta. It didn't occur to me that twenty-four hours later I would be packing up for a move toward the Sinai.

Sunday, June 4, was the last day before the war. If I refuse to call it the last day of "peace" it is because I don't consider the 1948–1967 period to have been a peaceful one. Internally, for more than a year now, we had been told we could relax. Eshkol's government had won the elections on slogans such as "The people are tired," and "Away with the activists." The Ben Gurion–Dayan–Peres members were presented as opportun-

28

ists who were using an imaginary security situation to obtain votes and power. Professional peace lovers promised us that with this group in opposition the chances to reach peace would be greater. "The people are tired," it was time to live a normal life unbothered by our Arab neighbors, and as Eshkol put it—to wear slippers instead of boots. Perhaps Nasser believed we had switched to slippers and that the only desires of our young people were for relaxation and the TV set. Fortunately the regular army knew how far we were from that desired security.

But Sunday was the last day before the war, and the country was back in boots. The press was demanding immediate action, the regular army through its commanders had assured the government and the people of its ability to win, and the activists, because of pressure from the "tired" people, were now in key positions. Dayan once said he would rather advance running in bare feet than walk in slippers. We were barefoot perhaps but we were able to advance fast. Not knowing we were to move that night, I had agreed to take care of some visitors to our division. Paul Shutzer, *Life* magazine photographer and a good friend, was visiting an infantry battalion; Bill Maulden appeared in the war room at Shivta and I joined him on a trip to Ktziot, to Castel's battalion.

Castel had a problem which he spoke to me about. In each platoon in the battalion there were a few reservists whose standard—mostly for health reasons—was lower than the others. They could not keep up the pace on the marches, and walking—fully equipped in the dune area—was the most important thing demanded of our infantry there. He had assembled them all into a special company and made them train with their doctor, who demanded less of them and hoped to help them reach the required standard. I saw the company sitting in the shade and joined them. Moshe had breathing difficulties, Fitousi was asthmatic, Nicolai was overweight, Yom-Tov had back pains and was wearing a corset, Amram was still recovering from an accident. Yom-Tov was crying like a baby; his tears mixed with the sweat and dust. They all had one complaint: They wanted to be back with their units. They would make an extra effort, they would not be left behind, they were as good as the others, and they refused the special classification given them. They were not young—"Our officers are our children's age," they said—but they could make it. "We are orthodox but we train on Saturday," one said. "Just let me go back to the company." Castel tried to explain to them. "You are my responsibility. I have to know what you are able to do so I want the doctor to watch you when you train." They refused to understand. We left them with tears in their eyes. Normally, in their reserve service, those people would have been delighted to have it easier, but it was the mood of the regular army which was contagious, which inspired their readiness and devotion. I walked with Maulden to one of the fortified hills.

The men were back from a shooting contest and were resting in the trenches. A singer who was in the *Fiddler on the Roof* cast made coffee for us in an empty tin and an Indian Jew, nicknamed "Bombay," decided in our presence to name his bazooka after his wife. Castel had to tell them that all leave was canceled but neither he nor I suspected—it was midday—what the reason was. Their daily routine was simple. From 3:30 A.M. they were all in a state of readiness—a dawn attack was still a daily possibility. They slept again from seven to nine and had breakfast at nine. Nine to eleven were hours of training, fortification, contests, and eleven to two rest again. Two to seven in the afternoon were hours of training, mostly marching—they did ten kilometers a day, fully equipped. At night, in rotation, 50 per cent of the soldiers were on watch, in ambushes or in a state of readiness in the trenches. "Nasser is giving us a paid vacation," someone said. "Kokos" was singing in Italian, Kadosh in Greek; "Bombay" said India was hotter but the food was spicy; Shuli washed Castel's laundry in an empty ammunition crate; Bill Maulden was taking pictures. We had a well-cooked lunch and returned to Shivta. I still didn't notice any particular commotion.

I slept in the tent for a couple of hours and with sunset I knew. Nobody said to me, "We are going to war." Helicopters landed occasionally and the war room was busy. We had to ask Maulden to return to Beer-Sheba and Dov said to me, "You had better get some equipment." We went to the supplies tent. I changed my boots for a better pair and got a new water bottle. The supply truck had now been stocked with items which had been missing earlier in the week and obtained at the last moment, and I took for myself a rucksack and a map case and pad. Dov got a pistol without bullets and there were no submachine guns left. "You'll find one on the way soon enough," I was told. A friend gave me two pairs of woolen socks. Walking back to the tent, I could see trucks being loaded. David, Dov, Zeevale, and I began to pack. I gave my identity cards to David and received instead a "prisoner's card." These were the details I was allowed to give if I was captured: Number 375963, rank—lieutenant, blood type, vaccinations, name, and family name—an uneasy one in my case. The card was placed in my pocket to join Omri's flower, dry by now, and Kuti's arrowhead. My identity discs had my name, number, and blood type and a gold chain with a star of David hung with them. I did not remove my two rings—a sapphire and a Greek signet ring, nor my gold chain bracelet. David packed clean underwear, two blankets, and a change of uniform into a small bag. Zeevale took the bag he came with—as it was—and Dov was writing letters in a corner while waiting for the driver to return with ammunition for his pistol. I tried on my helmet; it felt uncomfortable and heavy. Dov reminded us not to forget to take toilet paper. For how long? I asked. A week, at least.

The small light in the trailer was on but Arik was asleep on the wooden bench. He was stocking up. The cook was loading rations on the command car and I was quietly and persistently nagging Dov to make sure that once we moved I re-

31

mained with Arik's headquarters, and would not get left behind with the rear headquarters, as I feared might happen. I
finished packing. A bottle of cologne, a bottle of whisky, moisturizing cream, chocolate, writing paper, a change of uniform
and a Bible. I took a bathing suit—wherever we were going
we were bound to reach water—the sea to the north, the
canal to the west, or the Red Sea in the south. I wrote a
couple of letters—business ones. I did not feel the need to
write anything personal. Dov was writing to his brother and
we left the letters in the Lark for the driver to post. We left
the bags we did not intend to take along and went for a
drive. He was not nervous, just a little excited. "You'll see," he
said, "war strips you of all the superfluous. What remain are
the little immediate comforts—water in the canteen, toilet paper, cigarettes. Are you worried?" "No. I don't think anybody
in the world, excluding my brother, cares much whether I exist or not."

We saw soldiers writing letters, some trying to sleep, others
eating and listening to the radio. It was a clear night. A touch
of sadness hung in the air among these people who were preparing for their possible destruction. Nobody mentioned the
words "war" or "attack." At the most they said, "Well, we're
about to move at last." I thought of my brothers, my mother.
I knew where my father was and knew he would know where
I was. I thought of Castel's group of disabled—were they
packing, too? Of Kuti and Motke and their men. I dramatized
war when my thoughts concerned others. I tried to register
their faces and wondered if they would last the week; but of
my own predicament I did not think. I felt free, healthy, fit,
and secure. A caravan of trucks was waiting loaded along the
road. Arik was up when we returned, and though his first reaction was "certainly not," he agreed to let me join his headquarters before going off for a last meeting in the war room.
To my surprise I managed to sleep for an hour, and when I
awoke I was told to put my things in the command car. I
threw in two blankets as well as my sleeping bag, my helmet,

and rucksack. Unwillingly I heard Arik talking to his wife on the phone. "Be calm," he said, "kiss the children for me—soon—don't worry," and, many times, "Shalom, shalom, shalom, shalom," a repeated word, meaningful suddenly, a last note.

At 1 A.M. I saw Arik shaving in the trailer, wash his face, examine himself in the mirror, enjoy the after-shave lotion. He asked me if everything was ready. "We are going to win a war," he said. He knew, he radiated confidence, he was almost happy. The frustration had gone. Reports showed their intent to attack and movement of troops confirmed it. Their gun was loaded and set to fire and it did not matter any more who pressed the trigger or who fired the first shot. Everything around us was an act of war and we were about to take up the challenge. A photographer joined me on the command car, the cook, a driver, a medic, Zeevale, and David. Dov had the jeep and Arik went in the Lark while we were on the asphalt road.

At 2 A.M. we left the camp for a rendezvous spot where Arik was to meet the brigade commanders. The Lark led with full lights, the others followed with no lights at all. Along the road west a good number of vehicles were getting organized, but a stranger would not have been able to tell that on the following day war would break out. At a crossroads just before Nitzana we stopped. Arik got out of the Lark, loaded his small rucksack and two blankets on to the jeep, and began conferring with Motke and Arie. Kuti and Uri joined them. I stood close enough, but preferred to remain in the background. There was a feeling of confidence, of men in their element, there was professionalism, and a touch of joy. I understood that Natke, the Centurion battalion commander, was to move first as soon as the order was given, Motke would follow with the rest of the armored brigade, Kuti's infantry was to wait until midday, and Uri's combined troops were to wait and hold the defense line until ordered to move toward Kseime. The drivers of the different brigade commanders wished each other luck. Rachamim the cook was dozing off in the car. The commanders shook hands and hugged one another and mounted the jeep. From now on it was the communication set that we depended on—and until the next meeting when the battles were over we were to hear these people's voices, see them from a distance, but they would be separated from us, surrounded by their forces and maneuvered by Arik's orders.

All the hours of planning and replanning, all the war-room activities, the Intelligence reports and preparations, could be noticed in the way these men shook hands. They knew what it was all about; then the night swallowed them as they dispersed in different directions. The loess track we followed was like a white ribbon and we needed no lights. When we reached our marked spot we stopped. We were to wait there until the morning. The order, or rather green light, to move was expected around eight; it was now 4 A.M. The advanced headquarters was to move with the forces. It was also equipped to defend itself and was composed of three half-tracks. One was fully closed—the communication room, one was Arik's, the third was the artillery command. There were two jeeps with machine guns mounted in front, two smaller jeeps, and the supply command car. I was the only woman in this group. According to orders, the minute we stopped the men would start digging trenches. Arik asked me to wake him up at six-thirty and, bundled in a flight jacket, he lay on the ground between the half-tracks and fell asleep. Dov disappeared with his sleeping bag and I sat against the chains of the half-track next to Zeevale, resting but not sleeping. Behind us, moving west, I could see a cloud of dust—the familiar sign of armor advancing in the desert.

The sun mounted gently, painting us gold and waking up the men, who took off their pullovers and folded their sleeping bags. At six-thirty I woke Arik and asked him when he wanted his breakfast. I established the fact that I was going to help in our field kitchen and woke Rachamim to make tea.

To my horror I discovered that he had brought only half a loaf of bread, very few fresh supplies, and half-a-dozen eggs. It was going to be our last good breakfast, and on a blanket on the hard sand I set up a breakfast table: Fried eggs, sardines, cucumbers, bread, and some cheese and tea. When breakfast was prepared, I listened to the seven-o'clock news. Nothing was said. The price of gasoline was up as from today, the vice president of Egypt was going to Washington in two days, the three new ministers were to be sworn in in the afternoon, and the weather was going to be fair, maximal temperature in the south—29 degrees.

Breakfast was good. Arik, as usual, asked me whether I had eaten; he looked as if he had slept a long night in a comfortable bed. At seven-thirty we were told to be in a state of readiness. The men put on their helmets, so did I. I had no trench, and I watched the medic and the cook settle in theirs. I remained behind the half-track, writing an "eve of war" article. At seven-forty the generator was operated and the communication system started working. Something proved wrong in Arik's half-track and a part was changed.

Dov woke up, too late for breakfast, and over tea told me our big battle would be on Abu-Ageila. He reminded me that it would be a tough objective, that in the Sinai campaign in 1956 we had made many mistakes in our attempts to conquer it. In 1956 our forces had not combined to direct a single blow but had operated separately, without recognizing sufficiently the nature of either the area or the target. Arik, Dov, and others had been with the paratroopers in the Sinai in 1956 and they projected a feeling of here-we-go-again. "A strange way to go to war," someone said, "daylight, midmorning, just like this." It wasn't just like this, I thought. It was the only thing left to do. Both sides could make the first move in, the enemy moved, the straits were blocked, all the gates closed, and the people—an army. It was not at all "just like this," it was nineteen years of trying to believe that the Middle East would accept our presence, nineteen years of building what we were about to defend—it was all those moments of holding back, of being threatened, of being condemned and being left alone. At eight-ten, in a strong, confident voice, Arik gave the order to Natke, Motke, and Arie: "Nua-Nua Sop," which means "Move over," the two words we were ready for. At eight-fifteen we could see our tanks descending from the hills south of us toward the frontier and at eight-thirty Arik was watching with his binoculars and saying, "Here! We're shooting!"

The static period was over and the movement began. "Static" doesn't mean lifeless, for it had been a period of building and reinforcing, a phase both uncomfortable and inevitable. At eight-fifteen on June 5, we gambled all we had. What for other countries would have been defeat, for us would mean extermination. There was no way to lose the war and survive, and each man carried this knowledge along when we moved west—some with a sense of history and cerebral analysis, others with the primitive and powerful drive for self-preservation. The radio started broadcasting military marches, and the first announcement was made to the public—"From the early hours of the day fierce battles are taking place between the Israeli air force and armor and the Egyptian army which moved toward us." I felt stripped of everything now. Nothing much existed away from the immediate. We were moving, war was on, I was surrounded by men who were bound to win. The long wait was over.

The War

MONDAY, JUNE 5

I deserted the command car and climbed on the artillery group half-track. The wireless set was operating and it took me a while to get accustomed to the code words, combat terminology, and voices of commanders. Our main target was the defended locality held by the Egyptian 2nd Division—Um-Katef. The battle was planned for that night, and during the day our forces were to approach it, destroying on the way several outposts and opening the road to give our infantry fast-and-easy approach. In 1956, those outposts fell relatively fast and now we attacked them in several directions.

The Centurions, proud and streamlined, passed near us waving and turned to the dune area—flanking from the north to approach from the rear. Motke's tanks were to move along the asphalt road and be ready by nightfall to launch the main attack. Two other forces infiltrated southward in order to block the southern road to Um-Katef and prevent the arrival of support. Uri remained with his troops on the defense. The Centurions met the first "danger" or defense fire from one of the outposts and we moved to a higher point from which we could see our forces moving. For a while I felt as though I were watching a game. Tanks dispersed in the area, shells heard and seen, the wireless set like a background running commentary—there was something unreal about it all. I took off my helmet and listened to the radio. My father was talking to the soldiers. His voice was strong and clear—"Soldiers of Israel. . . . They are greater than us in numbers, but we will hold them. We are a small nation, but we are determined. We seek peace, but we are ready to fight for our lives and our country. . . . On this day our hopes and our security are with you." We were moving now.

I was standing in the half-track and looked at Arik standing in the half-track ahead. A cloud of dust signaled us and we rode fast. Words considered conventional on other occasions had meaning now, almost a biblical one. He was talking to Natke's boys in the Centurions slowly working their way toward an unmarked minefield, to the Sherman drivers in front of us answering the fire of Tarat-Um-Basis, an outpost, to Arie's swift AMX tanks in the south, to "Bombay" and Albaz, to me. At ten thirty-seven we crossed the green line. A border stone to our right—a heap of black and white bricks shaped like a connus, and the deserted U.N. patrol track. We were abroad.

The same loam dust, the identical terrain, the scorching sun burned just as much, but it was the other side, another country, enemy's land. No border police, no stamping of passport, no duty-free shops and vaccination cards—just so: a lift to the other side, a good-luck greeting, and we were in Egypt. In a few minutes we hit the asphalt road. The road I'd regarded as a hostile mystery now was ours, and we moved along it as if going for a ride toward Tarat-Um-Basis where the battle was on. The reports on the radio were good. Observation posts were evacuated, and a few enemy tanks and vehicles destroyed. Natke's Centurions had it tougher. Their approach was hardly passable. He lost a regiment commander and two company commanders and continued to attack the 181st outpost north of Um-Katef. I heard him asking for an air support as he was under heavy artillery fire stuck in mined dunes. He

38

was ordered to retreat and reorganize himself. A cousin of mine, David, was with the Centurions. "We lost seven tanks on mines," he told me, "but somehow I didn't feel it could happen to my division. After my tank destroyed its first T-34 we knew we were better and we needed the short rest not as a retreat but in order to reattack successfully in the afternoon." Shortly after eleven the outpost on the road—Tarat-Um-Basis—was in our hands and at noon we drove in.

It was my first encounter with an enemy post. Although we were warned of mines we climbed down. Every object held a special significance. Later we got used to the thrown kit bags, the vehicles, the burning tanks, the details of equipment, but there and then we treated them like children discovering a new world. Motke, who was a few kilometers ahead of us on the road, came over with a few captured guns and items and we touched them with awe. He unfolded a gas mask. I had never seen one before and only then the possibility of needing one dawned on me. Every Egyptian soldier had a gas mask and I looked at it wondering what they told about us. Soldiers walked around with cocked guns entering the few tents and making sure no enemy soldier was left around and we drove down in the jeep toward our Shermans who held the front line waiting for nightfall and occupying the enemy artillery from Um-Katef. At twelve-thirty four light airplanes appeared as air support—our "Fuga" training jets. With a sense of pride and comradeship we watched them diving north of Um-Katef. By then we knew that the Egyptian air force had been destroyed and neutralized in the early hours of the morning, and anything that had to do with air force was followed with looks of gratitude.

We didn't have to watch the sky wondering "Whose were they?" we didn't have to worry about the villages and towns in the rear—the sky of the Middle East was almost entirely ours. On the western slopes of Tarat-Um-Basis we stopped. An armored troop carrier was parked alongside the road. Dov entered it and came back with some papers and notes which must have constituted the payroll of a battalion. I entered a field tent which must have been used as a listening radio station—dirt, flies, a bowl of rice, dirty clothes. Dov gave me a packet of cigarettes "Belmont," my first Egyptian cigarette; "Hope they are not poisoned," someone said. We forgot about lunch that day and drove on in Arik's track to see the burning T-34 near the road. The sight of destruction somewhat bothered me. It all seemed so simple. True, Natke's battalion was hurt and had to retreat, but they were somewhere north of us and out of sight. Right here was the road, the deserted outpost, our own soldiers examining Russian machine guns and trying to start the vehicles; chewing hard rations, biscuits. Artillery fire heard from the west didn't seem to be directed at anybody in particular and the black asphalt stretching toward our Nitzana was already crowded with incoming vehicles carrying ammunition, gasoline, and supplies.

A giant yellow bulldozer of the engineering unit was fixing the road—filling a large hole formed by explosives when the enemy retreated, and shortly after one o'clock Arik ordered the infantry and Kuti to join us from Nitzana. One of the problems had to do with a lack of suitable transport for infantry. The infantry was to move in busses—a solution that was far from satisfactory—along the asphalt road, as far as possible, and walk the last twelve kilometers until nightfall to set up for the night attack.

The sun was inclined west now, and visibility toward the enemy was poor. The sight east was breathtaking. The road looked like a highway on a holiday. Bumper to bumper, vehicles moved safely with the caravan of busses—in their original colors of blue and turquois, original signs of "Egged-Tours"—carrying the infantry brigade. The danger was obvious; they were fully exposed and blocked in. The advantage—they arrived rested and fresh to the farthest starting point. I looked at some of our tanks and soldiers. The war had started that morning but their looks had changed completely.

The tanks were painted with slogans—"Express to Cairo," "Nitzana–Suez," "To Egypt with love," and improvised flags were hoisted to the tops of the antenna poles. The shaved, childish faces of yesterday gained a new sparkle. It was a winning army after its first contact, not yet in its supreme test but with all the confidence in the future. Talks about "a long and costly war" weren't heard, they knew the night battle would be decisive, they knew they had to win it, and they knew that it would crack the core of the Egyptian defense in the Sinai. Natke announced shortly after three that he was ready for a second try on his target, now with a support force which joined him, and twenty-five minutes later the outpost was in his hands. Itzik in a helicopter indicated the mines for them, six tanks managed to get into the outpost, and several T-34's were destroyed in tank-to-tank battle. The battalion refueled and moved on to form a blockade on the northern approach to Um-Katef. The radio was feeding us news of other fronts. We heard of air attacks by the Syrian air force on Natanya and Megiddo, and the early afternoon news described the shelling of several sections of Jerusalem. The busses with their load of an infantry brigade arrived, and a few minutes later the brigade was ready to go. Arik returned from talking to them, his face lit with enthusiasm—"What a sight!" he said. "These youngsters marching as if on the annual march to Jerusalem. A long column of soldiers, there isn't anything they cannot achieve!" The forces were dispersed now to their pre-battle positions and with sunset we, too, moved to one of the hills west of Um-Katef to await nightfall and the order to strike. "H" hour was fixed for 2200, and while the forces were forming up in a ring which was dead ground to the enemy I had plenty of time to gather information concerning the battle confronting us.

It was cooler now, and washing my face enabled me to forget I hadn't slept the night before. Being the only woman around created a natural difficulty when I was in need of a lavatory, and I walked in the dark feeling fully exposed against the whiteness of the soil. I put on a pullover and had something to eat, Rachamim made tea which we distributed, and Arik, still glued to the radio and checking over and over with the scattered forces, never forgot to thank me and add a couple of sentences. This time he said, "We are facing quite a battle, perhaps the most complicated one the army has ever fought." I sought Dov. He drew a map on a piece of paper for me illustrating the positions confronting us. All I could see in the dark were illuminating bombs which brightened the sky and were nervously sent up by the enemy from the moment darkness set in. Their artillery shelled aimlessly, and I was amazed how fast one's ears get accustomed to the sound. Dov drew a few lines on the paper. "It is a typical Russian defense system," he said, "composed of three straight lines, the outer one, the main, and a rear. The outposts cover an area of fourteen to fifteen kilometers. Their purpose is observation, warning, artillery observation, and delaying. Ideally, they could hold up the attack on the main defended locality for at least twelve hours, the advantage gained. In the case H hour is during the day, the main attack has to be postponed to nighttime when air support has to be given up and the armor efficiency is low. If H hour is for the night, the attacking force will find itself engaged in the main battle during daylight and then the attacker is exposed to all the guns and rifles and tanks." These outposts were now behind us and the risk of losing air support and visibility was calculated and accepted. Dov drew three long lines on the paper, crossing the road. "This is Um-Katef.* The lines are the long ditches, three of them resting confidently on the impassable dunes on the left flank and on high ground on the right flank. But there is no such thing as impassable ground. In front of them and among them are mines, and well protected in them is the infantry—a brigade, I figure. This is a powerful human and

* "Abu-Ageila" and "Um-Katef" refer to the same defended locality, Abu-Ageila being a small settlement on the crossroad defended by Um-Katef.

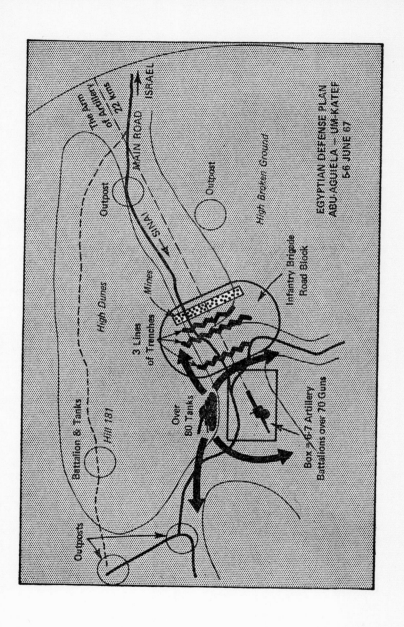

EGYPTIAN DEFENSE PLAN
ABU-AGUEILA — UM-KATEF
5-6 JUNE 67

physical block on the road." I tried to imagine them. Soldiers sitting in the ditches awaiting us. Do they make coffee in empty tins? Do they listen to Cairo radio bragging victories? Do they sing or chat or sleep? Our infantry brigade was walking now. Their job was to clear these canals marked on the piece of paper. Kuti was leading them. I felt the arrowhead in my pocket.

"Behind them is the artillery," Dov continued. "Between five and seven battalions. They constitute the long stretched arm able to hit far beyond the locality." I didn't have to wonder what they were up to. I could hear and see their action. Yaakov, the commander, had six battalions under command, including heavy mortars, field-gun battalions, heavy 160-mm. mortars, and medium guns. Only parts of his units were self-propelled and he was in position early enough for ranging properly; but he didn't have range enough to hit the enemy artillery although he advanced his guns as close as possible to the defended locality. So somebody had to go quickly and knock out the guns, not giving them a chance to halt our attack and to disperse their fire plan, and force them to engage us at unexpected directions. This task was given to Danny's paratroopers force. They would land behind the enemy lines and attack the guns from the rear. The third element in the Um-Katef defense system was the mobile dynamic one, the tanks. As known later—there were 90 of them, and if the infantry fire was local and pinned down to the trenches, and the artillery long ranged, the tanks constituted an active, swiftly moving fist able to hit in and around the locality, come to the aid of a threatened part of the locality, closing up a gap, stopping a penetration. Facing them were our tanks and armored infantry, Natke waiting on the northern approach to come in from the rear, and a Sherman battalion directly in front of the defense lines coming in from the east, on the main road. Their mission was to meet the enemy tanks as soon as possible and destroy them.

The lines on the paper grew vivid as Arik and Yaakov were

talking to the various commanders. When Dov said "heavy mortars" I could hear the never-tired voices of their men. When he described our armor, I heard Sason announcing he was shelled at but not in range; and at 19.00 with the last light, we could see the helicopters transporting the paratroopers to their assembly zone. Arik's voice changed some when he talked to Danny the parachutists' commander. He had been the commander of the paratroopers before, still wore a red beret, and they were his boys. He knew them all by first name and they were his men, and somehow he gave me the feeling he was talking to a brother in whose hands he entrusted a hard job. It was all clear now: the ditches, the artillery, and the 90 tanks awaiting us; and our plan—approaching from flank and rear unexpected, from the front along the road and enabling the infantry to clear the canals.

"What a difference from the Sinai campaign," an officer who fought here in 1956 said. "This time it is a real blow, all forces combined." Instead of testing and touching and going in drops, avoiding risks and softening up, this time Arik decided to concentrate the strike. Risk everything, perhaps, but stand the good chance of gaining everything as well. The idea was to attack from all directions, splitting the defense effort of the locality and occupying its three different forces at the same time, preventing them from supporting each other. On a different scale, this was the approach of the whole army in all fronts. For many days now I heard the terms "direct" and "indirect" approach. Ours was the indirect. The stronger hold was Kseime, and we were attacking Abu-Ageila–Um-Katef, supposing rightly that Kseime would fall as a result—either by trying to send support which would fall in the hands of our ambush or by retreating and deserting. The enemy defense plan and system were meant to force us into a "direct approach" of frontal attack by mining all flanks and relying on the geographical difficulties presented by the dunes in the north and the cliff in the south. We risked the armor in order to imply an indirect, unexpected approach and sent the tanks and the paratroopers from the dunes to the rear. As a direct approach would imply air support and visibility, we decided to go ahead with neither. What mattered in our calculation was not the amount of forces needed theoretically to take Um-Katef and open the main road in central Sinai, but the accumulative effect of a simultaneous attack from all directions at the same time. The fact that we were inferior in quantity was never a consideration.

The sky continued to be lit occasionally. H hour was near now, and the forces were waiting for the green light. The famous "silence before the battle" was evident in the hearts rather than in the air. Kuti told me later that "these were the difficult hours," lying on the sand and awaiting the order to go. Time to think, time to fear, time to wonder. "This is the hour of fear," he said, "never while in action, but just the moments preceding it." More tea, a walk to the edge of the hill. There was a windbreaker as it grew cooler, news broadcasts announcing continuous shelling on suburbs of Jerusalem, a sense of isolation, gratitude to the radio which, miraculously to me, tied us all together in coded chains of faith and strength.

We were told not to light a fire and had to improvise a cold meal. Toward ten o'clock I could sense an added nervousness. Commanders asked more often whether there were any changes. Arik was told there would be no air support, and the decision whether to wait until daybreak for support or launch the attack at night was left to him. He knew his people. He knew his enemy and the area, and his mind was made up swiftly. He was going ahead. H hour was postponed somewhat but just after 22.30 he gave Yaakov the order to open artillery fire. The battle had begun.

MONDAY NIGHT, JUNE 5–6

"Let everything tremble," Arik ordered. "Tremble it will," Yaakov answered. He ordered his artillery group—all types of guns—to open fire, and the area did tremble. For twenty

47

minutes, aided by projectors and aiming at targets, 6,000 shells fell on Um-Katef. The transceiver was busy. "Battery 2 to commander—two direct hits." "Well done, give them some more," corrections, occasional change of range, the sky lit as in a fun fair, and Arik rubbing his hands. "Such a barrage I've never seen." The two half-tracks were parked near each other and the commanders could talk, not using the net. Voices hoarse by now, Yaakov was reporting to Arik, who instructed all our other forces to prepare for the move once the artillery softening fire was over.

"It was quite a sight," said the paratroopers who were then on their way from the north toward enemy artillery positions. They landed in helicopters from eight-thirty on and met artillery fire along their track. Movement was difficult at night and they needed longer than calculated to reach the road. Assembly time was longer than expected and traffic on the road made it difficult to identify artillery positions by their fire. Arik ordered Yaakov to stop the fire after Kuti told him over the radio that he was ready to move in and that he had enough "softening-up fire." He waived the ten minutes more of shelling that he was given according to the plan. The effect of artillery shells in the dunes and on concrete, dug-in bunkers is more psychological than real, Kuti was thinking, and he wouldn't like to give the enemy in the trenches a chance to get accustomed to the bombardment and to wake up from the shock. He thought of his own men round him all crouching like sprinters at the start, impatiently and eagerly waiting for the sound of the shot from the umpire's pistol. Control of our artillery now, to avoid shelling our own advancing infantry, was switched and given to Kuti. Motke, Danny, and Kuti reported they were closing in "in the shortest possible way."

The Infantry Attack

My heart was with the infantry. Somehow they were the most exposed and the ones to have to confront the enemy face to face. Shelling our enemy and bombing "it" was one thing

—there was a distance and the shells carried their deadly message to map references, to numbered points on a map. The gunners in the tanks were shooting at tank silhouettes, but to the infantrymen the enemy were real people, human beings; they had to "make contact" with the adversary, to look in his eyes, to be stabbed by the look of surprise and the shock and bewilderment and fear and recognition of death when he emptied his submachine gun at a distance of a few yards in the narrow, smelly trench. I know I would never be able to tell what went on in the hearts of my friends there, a mile away from me, waiting for the green light. I say green light, borrowing my images, from terms in our daily experiences at the wheel of the car in front of red traffic lights or from an athletic or sports event. But this isn't a sports event and we are not on Diessengoff Boulevard.

We were a mile away and just on the precipice of danger. A shell falling a hundred yards from us was just a warning finger that made you shiver for a second and covered you with goose pimples; but they were trapped in the close embrace of death—both of them—our Uzi and their Ali. How does one get up and run into enemy trenches, into the unknown maze of communication ditches, into the warm intimacy of deep, underground shelters, and throw himself against hungry, open-mouthed muzzles of rifles, machine guns, grenades, bazooka, waiting silently for their prey or spilling, hosing fire in all directions? I know our men didn't drink liquor to work up courage. There may be a few words from their section, platoon, and company commanders, but nothing more. There was only the will to fight for one's own life first and then, maybe, for one's own family, for the freedom of our nation and state which ceased being an abstract term. Why do I say maybe? Because one doesn't know until the moment of trial comes. The boys and men I met were no heroes, they were just like me, a bit scared, a bit confident, they argued over little things such as who was digging more and who was running first to get a meal or whose turn it was

49

to clean the machine gun. You may be a very good soldier or commander at fire exercises or maneuvers, but this doesn't prove a thing, this doesn't make sure you'll be brave in battle and become a hero. Will they find the strength to throw behind their backs all their dreams and longings for a good job, plans for a nice vacation, for all the thousand-and-one wishes that are buzzing in a human mind and jump into the threatening jaws of the trenches?

My thoughts stopped suddenly and my questions were answered by Kuti's voice coming through the radio. "We have reached the tip and are advancing in the trenches to the south. I'm ordering artillery to move their fire. Tell tanks to do the same." The men in the tanks some 300 to 400 yards away could see the red and green lights that our markers were carrying, running above the trenches. Hours later, when I talked to some of the men, they explained to me all the how's and why's: "All the pictures, movies, you may have seen of an attack on a fortified position, on a defense line, show you waves of soldiers running with rifles and sparkling bayonets charging straight on and into the ditch. Some get killed before they reach the line and others are blown up by mines. With us it was different. We left the minefield, about two hundred yards deep and two to three miles wide, for the jackals. Ofer was given the center and most difficult line, Dov's battalion had the first, and Joseph the third, a mile to the rear. All of us approached the trenches from the north or from the left flank of the enemy. We came there unexpected through theoretically impassable dunes. Ofer's battalion was moving in company columns. . . ." They weren't quite sure they'd find the very beginning and left end of the line and they were careful not to bump on the trenches from the front, head on.

The terrain was quite difficult for navigation in the dark and there were explosions all over the place. A 120-millimeter shell exploded right over the spearhead platoon and wounded four men. But the company commander Rani, who was at the

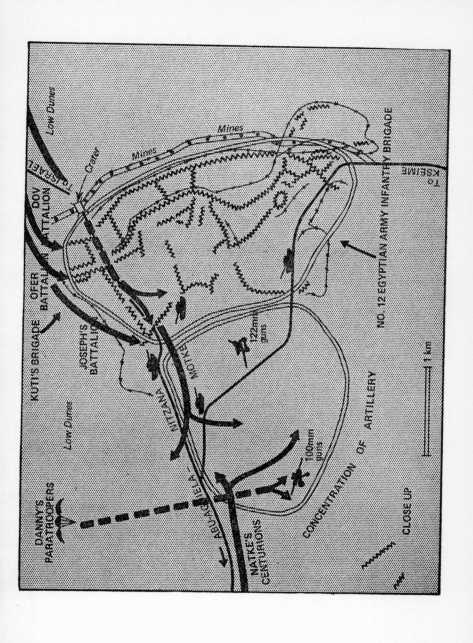

helm, pressed on and reached a low fence. A slightly wounded soldier threw himself over the fence and the whole company passed over his body. "There was fire from a bryanov machine gun and from several submachine guns but they were silenced within seconds, and the platoons jumped right at the beginning of the trench and started running inside throwing hand grenades before us, then running ten to twenty yards and squeezing the trigger of our Uzi submachine gun from the bends and corners of the communication trenches." The whole place was a labyrinth, a beehive of narrow concrete channels leading to concrete prefabricated round bunkers or to square niches in all directions. The enemy were taken by surprise. They were looking in front of them into the darkness of the night over the minefields, they were expecting us to run like goats and jump like rabbits over the mines and get blown to pieces. It is not theory or "maybe's" but we know it from the maps we captured and the words of the commander of a battalion who was taken prisoner in the battle —he was almost saying it wasn't a fair fight because we didn't knock on the front door and did not come through the locked gates of Um-Katef–Abu-Ageila. Instead, "we were running in their own sanctuary, along their corridors of power, facing them, tramping over their ammunition cases and mattresses and kit bags. Hitting them from the front and back in all sorts of positions."

At places there was stiff opposition, and it grew, and our pace was slowed. There were mix ups among our own groups. Dovalé's battalion got lost in the maze of trenches and came up facing Ofer's men, but small flicker lights prevented mistakes of identification. Ofer's G Company was running outside the trenches on the backbone of the ridge. C Company headed straight for the mortar positions just in the wadi, behind the line down the slope. They reached the road and a bit farther, after about an hour and a half of solid fighting. A platoon was left to hold the gap. It took another hour to reach the right end of the two- or three-mile long line. "Then we did

53

the whole thing backward just like you write Hebrew—from the right to the left, and collected our wounded. We got artillery and mortar fire on the positions we had just captured but it was silenced quickly by our guns. It wasn't easy going. The infantry had ten dead, two more died later of their wounds and about forty-five were wounded. The Egyptians had more than three hundred dead, about a hundred captured and wounded —we didn't have time to count them." We saw them early in the morning, our troops clearing and mopping up bunkers and distant positions and outposts, bringing in the wounded Egyptians, and carrying the dead. The place looked as if a hurricane had just struck—there were no victory cries, there was no jubilation, all men were tired and looked exhausted and aged. Only the machine guns mounted in the bunkers and the antiaircraft guns and mortars were shining in the early sun, indifferent, unmoved by what happened here to their masters.

It was more than a fair fight. It took all the courage there is to get into those ditches, well prepared, well dug in, with the enormous quantities of weapons of all sorts. They had all the material benefits—a good fortified position, abundance of fire power, even comfort. We had the bare necessities but spiritual superiority—the knowledge that we had to remove the enemy and that we knew how to do it. This type of fighting in a fortified position was a sort of "kabbalah"—a tradition or ritual secret handed over from the paratroopers, when Arik was still their commander, to all the small units of the whole army. This was definitely the "comparative advantage" our infantry achieved over the "competitor," just as we excel in growing the best oranges. It takes a lot of training to fight in trenches and at close range, but you have to have the ingredients in you. The Egyptian soldier just didn't have it in him; he was dependent. He relied on his officer, on the artillery, on the mortars, on his anti-tank platoon, on somebody or something outside himself.

"This is all nice and fine," a lieutenant told me, "but after you count your own dead and wounded, and you find and recognize among them a familiar face or hear of a name you know, there is no escaping the question: Was it necessary? Couldn't we do without this 'classical,' costly fight of infantry, in crude language, this simple, straightforward killing of people?" He was not questioning here the sense and necessity of the whole battle, just this part of it: couldn't the artillery and tanks and air force have won the fight by themselves? Perhaps, but almost certainly not. The effect of the artillery bombardment was negligible; it was frightening while it lasted, but wore off quickly. The enemy infantry in the trenches could have held on to their positions, even after air raid and strafing, and could have inflicted heavy casualties to tanks, had they tried to penetrate the defended perimeter before our infantry removed the human and physical obstacle from the road. But we have to go back to ten o'clock in the evening to the paratrooper attack.

The Paratroopers' Attack

Danny's force was put under our divisions command at the last minute. I used to see him come to the command wagon in Shivta at very odd hours to discuss plans for an hour or two and then helicopter away. Now, around half-past eight, his helicopter was over our heads. He was on his way to a landing place in the dunes some three miles to our west. Thousand-and-one tracer bullets were drawing on the darkness of the night an illuminated dome, and I was looking up at the planetarium-like sky searching for the helicopters. Their line of approach and landing place were changed just an hour or two ago. They were supposed to come in from the south and land on an elevated spot called The Dalafe, southwest of Abu-Ageila. But after the capture of the battalion defense block on the dune track by the Centurion battalion, they could fly in straight and unload the paratroopers just north of the enemy artillery concentration.

The force came in three waves, and it took them little time

to organize, but the enemy discovered the landing spot and started zeroing in. First only sporadic, single shots, and then around ten-fifteen a whole salvo right on the landing markings. Luckily three helicopters were about two hundred yards away in the air. The landing spot was moved away little by little so that by the time the whole force was assembled they found themselves much farther from the objective than was intended and had to walk quite a distance. The map defines the ground as "sharply undulating sand scrub," but it was an ordeal even for the tough and seasoned parachutists. It was like walking up a razor's edge, then coming down—and up again. They were divided into three groups of men, each of them headed for his own objective—a battalion of guns. They started out around ten-thirty and Levy's force attacked around midnight while the guns were still blasting away their load. Three batteries of field guns were silenced in a matter of minutes and the gunners of other antiaircraft guns abandoned their positions and started their run to the southwest. Levy's group met a few trucks coming from the main locality and some that were speeding reinforcement or supplies to the attacked force. A section attacked the trucks from close range and unfortunately blew up a few tons of ammunition in one truck—three were killed and three more wounded at this spot. The force had some twelve other casualties, and they were burdened with the wounded. Levy was permitted to concentrate his men and evacuate his wounded from the artillery locality back to the north of the main road half a mile outside the perimeter. Evacuation was quite an ordeal. Jud, one of the unit's two doctors, said: "I was scared until I had to treat the first wounded. From that moment on war became a job to be done. I have seen in hospitals people with less pain crying out and moaning. Here, soldiers lay legless, their hands crushed, a bullet in the neck, fragments in the stomach—without as much as a sigh. They were conscious and some refused morphine. I could talk to them. The dead were

General Arik Sharon on top of his half-track with officers.

Vered

Left. One hour before the war on June 5. Arik is up after a short sleep; I am writing my diary. *Above.* Arik addressing officers in the War Room. *Below.* A commander addressing his brigade—regulars and reservists—on Tuesday morning after the battle of Um-Katef.

Vered

Um-Katef defended locality. The road to Ismaelia
(horizontal line in the foreground) is protected
by three ditches held by an infantry brigade.

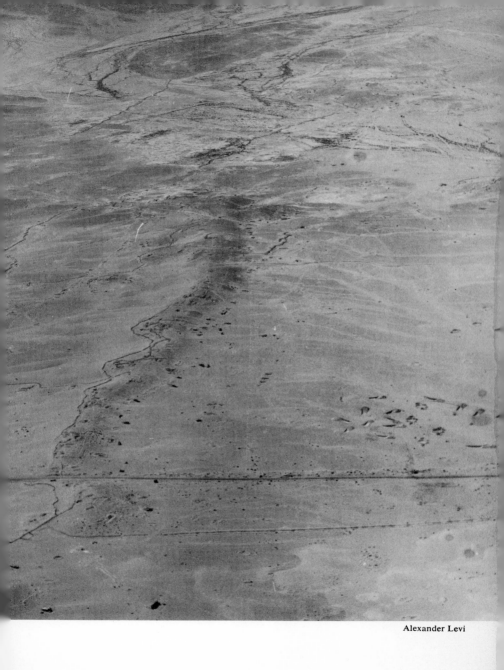

Alexander Levi

Vered

Above. Our armor on the road, dispersing into a formation for action. *Below*. Our headquarters convoy on the road. *Right*. The division's first prisoners. Um-Katef, June 6.

Alexander Levi

Above. Tuesday morning, after the Um-Katef battle, wounded Egyptians in one of the ditches. *Below*. One of the missiles found in the Sinai. Trying to escape, the vehicle was stuck in the dunes and destroyed.

Alexander Levi

Above. A Russian T-34 tank burning near Tarat Um-Basis. The first morning of the war. *Below.* A leftover of a huge Russian helicopter in Bir-Gafgafa airport in the Sinai.

Alexander Levi

Left. A postcard home from the battlefield in haste—before the helicopter takes off. *Above and Below*. Evacuation of the wounded by Air Force helicopters.

Vered

Above. Morning prayer in the field. *Below*. Between Abu-Ageila and Nahel. The newest Russian amphibian tank enjoying an Israeli crew. *Right*. Arik (left) and Dov in Nahel, leaning against the command half-track.

Vered

Vered

Left. Arik and I, after the Nahel battle. In background, Itzik the radio operator, and Katz the gunner. *Above*. Dov in foreground after Nahel's battle, Arik and I in background, Itzik the radio operator on the jeep.

A natural "facial" after the battle on Nahel —the last day of the war.

Vered

carried in blankets. We had only ten stretchers and some of the wounded insisted they could walk or limp along without help. The difficulty was to make sure the infusion needles stayed in place while we advanced under fire. The knowledge that the wounded were utterly dependent on me was at times unbearable. Who am I, after all?"

Who is Jud? One could hear from the paratroopers he saved. "I have never met a doctor like Jud. He worked under fire walking straight, mocking the bullets, holding a torch, and finding the time and presence of mind to extend beyond the medical treatment a comforting smile, a good word, a wink, a promise. He worked for eight hours without stopping, ignoring the danger, behaving in the battlefield as he would in a hospital in the rear. They had to wait for the helicopters until daybreak. Two men were dying and Gadi was in bad shape. 'Talk to him,' Jud ordered, 'don't let him fall asleep. If he falls asleep, he will never wake up.' Shlomo talked to him, and when Gadi shivered they took off their shirts and covered him. When the sun appeared in the east, Gadi opened his eyes. 'Am I still here? I thought it was the end. I think I can make it now.' 'Of course you will,' Jud told him. 'The sun,' Gadi whispered, 'don't hide it.' The helicopter arrived. Jud stroked the hair and forehead of his 'patients.' They were safe now. He himself thanks the battalion commander— He was God for me that night. Every word he uttered, be it the most casual one, inspired calm and confidence. He was my doctor."

Soldiers I talked to referred to friends as heroes, never admitting or realizing that their own acts were as distinctly heroic. They are always embarrassed by it. They shrugged and said—"Well, what do you expect? Should I have run away?"

The other two groups didn't get a chance to express themselves, because of the swift action of our two tank battalions. They succeeded in penetrating into the defended perimeter

57

earlier than planned and in order to avoid a mix up between our own troops, Arik ordered the paratroopers to give the tanks a clear field for action.

While walking back, the paratroopers cleared their way in the midst of Egyptian soldiers running and fleeing in all directions. They figured that in the attack on the guns some forty Egyptian gunners were killed and a few more on the way back to their concentration zone. Most of the Egyptian guns inside the locality were quiet by now. The paratroopers were crossing the main road on their way to rest and tend their wounded while the tanks took the field.

The Tank Battle

The whole afternoon Sason's Shermans were "playing" the enemy's defense plan game: letting him think we are going into a frontal attack according to his book. Sason, a tall, balding man looking like a new edition of Karel Salomon the conductor and composer, was taking advantage of the time introducing the enemy to his tank commanders. He called forward, in rotation, a few tanks from each company, showed them the enemy positions, let them have a pot shot at a tank, sent them back to the rear to refuel and store up ammunition. His observation posts were helping the artillery in ranging targets. The afternoon dust storm was making visibility poor. Add to it the dust from shells and movements of tank and vehicles and you get quite a blurred picture. Sason's engineers were repairing, meanwhile, the craters that were blown up by the enemy on the main road.

At the same time the other tank force—Natke's Centurions—were a few miles away to the northwest mopping up the battalion outpost on hill 181. Six of his tanks got inside the defense zone. There were about 20 T-34 tanks in there, some of them putting up a fight, but most of them leaving in all directions. About five T-34 tanks were knocked out. It was already dark now, and after some reorganization they started toward the Abu-Ageila–El Arish road. A small force was left

58

at the crossroad to block and stop eventual reinforcements coming from the north; (around midnight they did hear the roar of tracks from the north, but after a few signals on the identification channel it turned out to be "friend"—the forward units of Avraham Jaffe's tanks).

Another small force was left behind at Abu-Ageila to block aid from the west—Bir-Hasana or Gebel-Libni. Perplexed, wandering, indecisive enemy tanks were roaming on the road, along the road, on the sides, in opposite directions. About twenty of them were destroyed, one point blank from ten yards, after he was trodding along for five miles in our own column, either pretending he was Israeli or not knowing he wasn't among his own Egyptian tanks. Around two-thirty in the morning this force was coming in from the rear into Um-Katef–Um-Shihan defense perimeter, their guns quiet as ordered by the division, so as not to hurt the paratroopers who were just clearing out. Up to this moment this force was under the direct command of the division, but from now on they were to come under Motke, who was commanding the other armored units, to avoid contradictory orders and achieve a single reign over all tanks—for the last kill—the tank-against-tank fight.

Just after midnight Sason heard over his radio Kuti's voice telling Arik that his forces had crossed the main road along the trenches. Orders were given to Motke to get his men through the road. Sason's first four tanks got through. There was a very deep crater the width of the road closed by minefields on both verges. The fifth tank stepped on a mine, got stuck, and closed the gap. There was no way in but to clear a gap in the minefield. Zeevik came forward with his sappers.

It was taking some time, and Arik was getting impatient over the radio. This was, he thought, the most critical moment, the moment he could assure victory, to push his tanks inside the enemy defenses and wipe out the Egyptian force of ninety tanks minus five or six that were knocked out in the afternoon. Ninety tanks is a mighty big force and capable of annulling the achievements and success of the infantry and paratroopers. If well organized, and if well led in well-prepared dug-in positions and in hideouts, they could tip over the scales. Nobody knew how they would fight, but Arik gave them credit and the benefit of the doubt. Maybe the enemy was shrewd and waiting with his last trump card for the final blow and kill. Arik was pressing Motke to hurry up, and cool and calm Motke was telling him quietly all was going to be all right. "This was the only time," he said later, "that I told Sason to hurry up. Sason is a man always in a hurry and there was no need to push him." But it was taking time. Zeevik looked for the two flait tanks left some three miles behind. They were under Sason's command, given to him for two eventualities—in case Kuti's infantry would not be able to open a gap on the road or if the tanks would be sent forward, ahead of the scheduled timetable, during daytime—to break into the defenses. Nobody knew why they were left "so far" behind. My guess was, from what I sensed and knew of the character of the Israeli commander, that anything that was not actually fighting was pushed a bit behind.

While Zeevik, the commander of the engineer battalion, was searching for the flait tanks and picking them out from their hiding place and bringing one forward, clearing the road from blocking tanks, his men started picking up mines the old-fashioned way—by hand, like picking potatoes, this time hot potatoes, in the field. The actual clearing and widening of the gap in the minefield took only half an hour, but the whole operation took almost two hours. Zeevik didn't use his bungalor torpedoes which could have blown up the mines quicker because he wasn't sure our own troops and tanks would not be hurt.

All Sason's tanks started pouring into Um-Katef. They didn't shoot because they had to make sure first that the paratroopers were out of the way and that Kuti's infantry was protected—and because they had orders to look and search for their own match in tanks of the enemy and not waste their tank power on small fry. They were advancing steadily to the third line of trenches. One Sherman was knocked out next to the trench and caught fire, but the crew had time to escape; two more were hit on their tracks but managed to knock out their adversary; a fourth got it in his fuel tank but kept on fighting; a fifth and sixth were hit by heavy machine-gun bullets and by an artillery shell but nothing serious happened to them.

The two tank forces were closing in on the enemy, Natke from the rear and Sason from the front. Both of them were being fired at by anti-tank guns or tanks and both complained over the radio to Motke, the brigade commander, that the other fellow was shooting him up. Motke had a brain wave of Solomon's wisdom; he ordered Sason to stop all his tank guns from shooting and asked Natke if he was getting fire. He was, so Motke ordered him to shoot back. A few minutes later the same exercise was repeated the other way around. Sometimes they used their projectors to identify the tank before they shot. All of them remembered well "last time" in 1956, when at the same spot two of our tank forces—one from the 7th Brigade and the other from the 37th—clashed here at midday, the third of November, and in a matter of five minutes the 7th Brigade force knocked out eight tanks of their own brothers in arms from the 37th Brigade. Darkness lifted slowly before the two tank battalions met. Suddenly there was angry, rapid, shot fire and shots all over the place. We could hear and see the shots from our division command post—these were duels between "pockets" of resistance of Egyptian tanks, realizing they were caught between the two arms of our tank forces, trying to break free from their hug. Sason met seven tanks, T-34's. They were destroyed in a matter of minutes, one was burning, moving on toward Natke's tanks like a giant flaming torch.

Almost at the same time Natke reported one of the tanks was hit and was burning, the crew escaping, and then his radio went dead. He was hit and badly wounded in both legs.

Natke's radio operator, Yehuda, was hurt as well. In hospital, after the war, he remembered: "It was at five in the morning. We noticed the entrenched Egyptian force only when they opened fire. We tried to move away looking for shelter but it was too late and our half-track was hit by a T-54 tank's gun. I was operating the machine gun and I saw Natke being hit. I tried to help him, not realizing my own wound, but when I attempted to stand up there were no legs to stand on and I collapsed." Natke's second-in-command took over and carried on the fight with enemy tanks.

"To open the Nitzana–Abu-Ageila road for other formations—to fight the enemy tanks in the depth of Sinai," the second objective of the division read.

It was still dark when I turned my head left, to the east, and there, as far as I could see, were a thousand headlights moving on, advancing rapidly toward us, below on the main road. Arik was on top of his command half-track, raising and pointing his hand to the horizon as if blessing the sight, the moment. On the radio was Shaike, the general commanding southern command: "It's Jaffe's second armored brigade, make them pass you as quickly as possible." Hundreds of our own supply and ammunition trucks were moved in a matter of minutes away from the road, our own tank-brigade reconnaissance jeep took theirs, as if by the hand, and led them, full speed, the ten more miles through Um-Katef–Um-Shihan. The fight with the Egyptians was still going on, but the whole brigade sped through, without any hindrance, to fight the concentration of Egyptian armor on the second line of the defense of Sinai–Bir-Hasana and Gebel-Libni.

Our armor lost nineteen tanks in this battle, three half-tracks, most of them from Natke's force. Sason had to his unit's credit about thirty Egyptian tanks and Natke about the same number. Our tank forces lost eleven men.

Um-Katef–Um-Shihan was in our hands before time. It was a cursed place for us in 1956, in the Sinai campaign, and the commanders and officers who knew their history still remembered the fate of the 10th Infantry Brigade and the 37th Armored Brigade. Later, as I was filling in my diary with the details which I didn't have at the time, Dov shoved under my nose my father's diary of the Sinai Campaign: "Read, look what was going on in the back of our minds that night; read, and you will find out why Arik was so anxious to get the tanks in and why he was pushing forward relentlessly the whole time. I took the book and read: "I explained to the brigade command that Um-Katef had to be captured as quickly as possible. . . . It was essential to open a favorable axis of movement. . . . Um-Katef commands the only asphalt road which can serve our forces . . ."

There followed a description of the two attacks that failed:

". . . The first Battalion lost its way, failed to find the main enemy position, lost contact with its companies, tramped about the hills at night, etc. The 2nd Battalion, too, had difficulties in finding their objective, and after an arduous night of slogging up and down the resistant sand dunes they managed to get near the enemy position. . . . One platoon met with enemy fire, one man was killed and another wounded. That was the end of their attack. The Battalion withdrew."

Here the failure of the next attack is examined. "The first half-tracks went into a minefield . . . and went out of action. The command half-track was among the first to be hit."

My father counts all the mistakes that were studied and avoided this time. Faulty intelligence, lack of familiarity with the terrain, and an attack "which did not follow a sound operational plan which would give full battle expression to the entire strength allocated for this operation."

Later in the book he returns to it. "The defended localities of Abu-Ageila are the only sectors so far where the Egyptians fought extremely well and our forces extremely poorly. The basic fault in our fighting here is that it was done in dribs and drabs." (General Dayan, *Diary of the Sinai Campaign*)

I now understood why he was happy with Arik's plans. The Egyptians fought as well this time as they did then, but there were no dribs and drabs about our combined operation.

My father writes about the Egyptian fighting:

"The Egyptian forces fought well during the static phase of their combat. So long as they were required to use their weapons which had been dug into fixed positions in advance . . . they did so automatically, accurately, and efficiently. But this was not the case when they had to leave their entrenched posts or make changes in their plans. They carried out almost no counterattacks; and when they did, their action was pretty poor."

Our experience that night proved they hadn't changed. Tactically they were adequate; but when it came to a dynamic move, a change of strategy, taking initiative, or being inventive—they were hopeless. The division achieved its objective—it destroyed an important vertebra of the backbone of the Egyptian defense line. That morning we knew only that the immediate danger to Nitzana–Beer-Sheba was averted.

Little did we know that the war was won, that Sinai was ours, that the Egyptian army was a body without a soul, without a spirit, without a command. The bulk of the Egyptian armor was still in the center of Sinai, almost untouched —the whole of the 7th Tank Division, and a couple of armor brigades, over five hundred tanks still capable of putting up a fight in spite of the fact that their air force was almost nonexistent.

Arik was anxious to push on as quickly as possible for the next fight, before the enemy woke up, before one of their generals with initiative took over and put some guts in them. He refused to give them reprieve, respite. He demanded in radio talks with Shaike to be given new assignments. He offered to take Bir-Hasana.

TUESDAY, JUNE 6

Red eyes after another sleepless night adjusted to the first light of day. Men who were tied up to transceivers stretched and moved, and Arik's efforts were now concentrated on getting more helicopters for evacuation of the wounded. On the horizon we could see a thick cloud of dust and the first half-tracks and tanks of Avraham's division. "What a majestic sight," Arik said proudly. The night's battle was almost over and fresh forces could use the road to Abu-Ageila and farther west toward Ismaelia on the Canal. Our job here was done. We had given them a free entrance to the center of Sinai and just above them the first helicopters appeared. Rachamim was asleep under the command car. By now he knew my "let's make tea" smile, and I prepared breakfast. Arik shaved, and on a ridge overlooking the newly opened road with the endless line of vehicles on it, we had some canned sardines, biscuits, cold meat, and tea. Spasmodic fire could still be heard when Arik said, "We're going down." We mounted the vehicles and only then I realized how close we were to the battlefield, protected by the darkness and a few dunes.

We drove to the center of the location, among our tired soldiers, along the grayness of the end of battle area. The dunes were gray, spotted by shells' hits, shrapnel, and fragments covered the ground, sharp and gray, gray people, gray thoughts, blazing sun. We parked the half-tracks and descended. I looked for familiar faces. At first all faces looked alike—red eyes, a mixture of fatigue and sadness, a flicker of pride, anxious looks following the helicopters with their human load of wounded friends. Kuti appeared. Motke joined us. We hugged and embraced, and there was no need for

65

words any more. The abstract voices of night required their human physical entity. Worn out, unshaved, but satisfied. "No arrowheads here," Kuti said. He took a shrapnel out of his pocket. "Plenty of those, though. This is my personal one, almost did me in." "I have candies this time," I said, and gave him a pack I had. "Good girl. What are you doing here anyway?" We walked to his jeep. Someone was making coffee. "All I want is a ranch. Cattle, sheep, pasture," and as an afterthought, "Do you know, I never killed in war; not even tonight in the ditches?" Occasional shots were heard nearby. "It is Joseph, your friend," somebody said. "He is still clearing the third ditch." I thought of "Bombay," Kadosh, Cocos—his men. I remembered his reservists with the asthma and the corsets. They were clearing the bunkers now and Kuti just kept saying, "What an ugly thing war is. Now I hate it." I showed him the arrowhead and he smiled and walked away to join Arik and Motke. They climbed to an observation point to reconstruct the details of the night's battle. Apparently there were very few diversions from the original plan. I was standing on the head cover of a bunker. Below me was our army—refueling, resting, refilling water containers, eating. It was only then that I turned to look at the enemy or sense its destroyed presence. In the ditch leading from the bunker lay a corpse. My first contact with the dead enemy. I examined it closely, my boots almost touching the outstretched hand. He was small, dark, fine featured. His face was already covered with flies and his khaki uniform hung loosely over the dead limbs. Black blood covered his belly, and his head was bare, with black dirty hair. I had to admit an absence of feeling which grew in proportion to the number of corpses I saw. This one was more than an object but less than a human reality with desires and dreams and relatives who cared. He was a victim; his death was an inevitability; he was pathetic. My eyes left him and wandered along the ditch.

Two more corpses and a group of prisoners. Someone I knew was guarding them. They were officers. They looked better fed than the soldiers; they were older and as silent as the dead. "You should have heard Motke," the guard told me. "He lectured them in English as if they were his pupils in a cadet school. Lectured? He preached. He told them they should be ashamed of themselves. He told them they did not deserve an officer's rank. He pointed out to them the fear of their men, their lack of pride and devotion." One of the prisoners looked up at me. I met his eyes. Black, curious, pleading. Here it was. Nasser's promises and bragging, the threatening, choking political reality, the millions of dollars we invested in the army, the war songs and the arms, Kuti's thirteen dead of last night—this was the enemy defeated, frightened, reduced to a pleading animal, grateful for the water we gave him and hoping to survive. Was he promised Tel-Aviv loot and women? Was he told of our inferiority? Did he go to war believing, the way we did, that he was bound to win? Someone offered me "a cake from home." Only then did I realize the element of time. It seemed we were on the way for days, and the cake a piece of memory from a distant past. Into twelve hours were crammed more sensations than in weeks, raw, confused, pushed aside to be digested later, all new. "What can I give you?" Kuti asked me. "I think I would like a gun." He walked over to a pile of weapons collected in the area, tried several, and chose one. "Here, you may have it. I don't think you need use it." Some prisoners were lying down, face in the sand. A few curious soldiers surrounded them, hardly commenting, never teasing or bullying, just watching. Did they think of friends who died that night? Did they compare themselves to them? Did they want to see the enemy who at night was a jaw of a machine gun throwing fire? There was no hatred in their eyes. A touch of contempt perhaps, and a touching wonder. Smoke grenades were thrown occasionally to mark landing spots for the helicopters and I walked back to our headquarters, stopping to look at the loading of wounded. What remain of battles are always heroic episodes. Little is written about the dirt and the flies, the fear and the agony. Yet it would be unjust to dismiss the heroism of our wounded for the sake of not being banal.

Medics and doctors, who worked miracles under fire, were amazed at their behavior. "Not in the war of independence, not even in Sinai, were the wounded so brave." The infantry doctor told me of soldiers who hid a serious wound until morning so as not to be evacuated before the battle was over. The sentence "Treat him first, I can wait," was a common phrase used by them all, and their sense of humor and high morale didn't leave even the dying. Doctors carried on in spite of their own wounds, treating enemy soldiers as well as their own, and with a last bit of strength those who were evacuated smiled to us from the stretchers.

The ten-o'clock news announced the victory in Um-Katef and the Jordanian retreat from Latrun, Nebi Samuel, and Jenin.

Our half-tracks were refueled, we had a fresh supply of water and were ready to go. "Where to?" I asked. "Along the road south where we shall stop for the night and await instructions."

I moved from the artillery half-track to Dov's jeep where I was to stay through the remaining days of the war. It was a good change. Somehow the speed and size of the jeep gave me a sense of security. Dov was a brilliant driver and jeep driving in this area was not an easy task. What from a distance looked like smooth terrain proved to be a broken ground. One had to drive along contours, modify the acceleration when stuck, choose a track avoiding the deep tracks of heavy vehicles and tanks on the road, and keep the jeep steady and fast. In a few minutes we were leading the headquarters convoy. With us on the jeep, as a permanent crew, were Katz, a gunner and a reconnaissance soldier, and Itzik, a radio operator. Our transceiver was open and we could hear all communications. We had a good set of maps, the machine gun was loaded, and we had a container of water and K-rations. Driving meant very little dust and I felt I could go on like this forever. Along any road, in any direction. At this stage we were still looking with a touch of excitement at every destroyed vehicle of the enemy. We were heading south and leading the division when Arik suggested we stop. In our footsteps arrived the armored brigade and we moved on a few miles to a hill left of the road where we parked for the night. The forces were moving on, along the bad road, to stop a mile or so ahead. We sat and watched them, tank after tank, jeeps, half-tracks, command cars. They waved and drove on in whirlpools of dust. The dust didn't matter any more; somehow it didn't feel like dirt. I longed for the moment I could take off my shoes and socks but felt physically better than ever. The afternoon news broadcast announced the city of Gaza was taken and described the shelling of several kibbutzim by Syrian artillery. Yet we felt isolated. I was anxious to get news of other fronts but didn't have a feeling that we were a part of a total war. There was the division, behind it the rear headquarters, and the logistic branches, behind them was Shivta, the Lark with our belongings, and home much farther. The war until now was a day of advance, a night of battle, and today—its aftermath. Ahead was the road, the next target, the wilderness of Sinai, and perhaps a few hours' sleep. Right there the war was our war, and breaking the sense of isolation were the air-force actions in our area and the division which drove through Um-Katef in the morning, westward.

I prepared supper. Heated cans of goulash, peas and sweet corn mixed, slices of apple in syrup, and tea. We could hear and clearly see shells falling from the direction of Kseime but I was too tired to register. With darkness, small log fires appeared and the site looked like a gypsy camp. I managed to wash my face and arms and behind a low hill changed my shirt. I succeeded in combing and rebraiding my hair and even applied some moisturizing cream to my face and neck. Itzik and Katz were asleep in the jeep, cuddled in blankets, and Dov and I took our sleeping bags to a group of desert bushes between the vehicles. The hard white surface felt like the softest of beds once I took off my shoes and zipped myself in the bag. I don't think I managed to say good night. We had had no sleep for sixty hours now.

WEDNESDAY, JUNE 7

We were as good as new in the morning. A short discussion resulted in agreement that it *was* Wednesday, and while the men were washing I prepared breakfast. Breakfast menu never left much chance for surprise. Pickles, sardines, biscuits and jam, tea and cold meat. We ran out of canned fruit salad but I discovered a crate of Jaffa oranges for export under the blankets and guns and boxes in the command car. The sight of the oranges this morning won me smiles and gratitude as if I had succeeded in growing them overnight. I put on a khaki shirt which was sleeveless, sleeves removed by a pocketknife, and under a bush set up the food. Arik and Dov were looking at the maps and Arik was awaiting information and instructions. "I would like to go west," Arik said. "Will you take me to the sea? Any sea?" "I promise," Dov answered. A jeep pulled toward us and Kuti appeared. We had said good-by in Um-Katef and his arrival was a good surprise. "Want to go for a swim?" he asked. He was taking his brigade north, to El-Arish. "You can't have her," someone said. "We'll reach water, too, sooner or later, and meanwhile we've got to eat." Arik was called to the radio and returned suggesting we were to head south. Sharm-El-Sheikh. When the tea was hot and ready, he was called again. "We are off soon. We'll follow the track south toward Nahel. There are several enemy concentrations along the way."

Kuti left us. Walking infantry was useless for our task and we were a smaller division now. While we started moving south, Uri's force entered Kseime. My reservist friends from Bari's battalion descended from the Little Sabcha, and climbed the Big Sabcha in twenty-five minutes. They had no vehicles and walked along the asphalt road to Kseime. At ten o'clock they

70

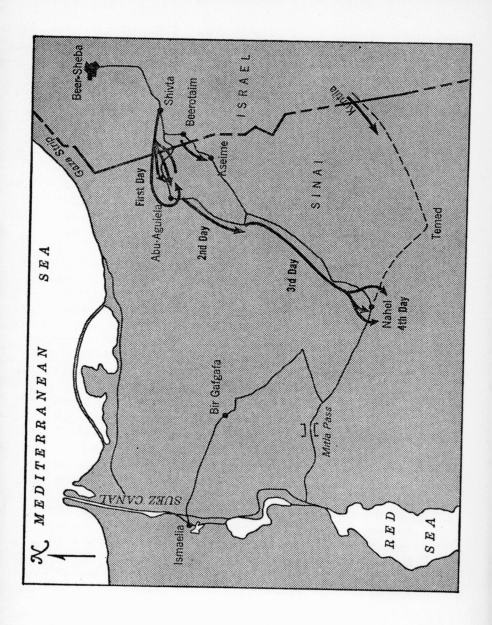

reached Kseime, facing the third minefield along their advance route. They entered Kseime to find no resistance. The locality was evacuated and the few remaining soldiers were killed or captured. A Piper Cub coordinated Uri's people with our armored infantry battalion which entered Kseime from the rear, and after reorganization Uri moved his forces toward our axis of movement. The enemy used last night to retreat from Kseime. Our forces caught up with some of them later, but we didn't succeed fully in blocking their retreat because of fatigue, misunderstandings, communication problems, and the fact that the service echelons were late in catching up with the armor which was left without fuel. Now we were on the move again. If ever I thought the Negev was a real desert it took the Sinai wilderness to prove me wrong. The Negev was intimate and friendly in comparison. Here it was larger than life and deadlier than death—as far as the eye could see. Monotonous, colorless, hostile. To our east was Kadesh Barnea. I wondered were my father there would he have stopped and driven over to do some digging. We said nothing, but we were conscious of the fact that we were covering backward the route Moses took. "And the people abode in Kadesh; and Miriam died there." Here "Moses smote the rock and water came out abundantly." Here they were refused entrance to Edom and had to bypass it and travel down to the Red Sea. Here Karah rebelled and God's wrath sent the plague down. Arie was leading with the tanks, followed by Sason's armored battalion and the headquarters, when we reached a plateau and a crossroad. The road from Kseime to Bir-Hasana, east to west, was before us, and to our right was a defended locality called Abirik. Arie reported that the axis he was on—a few miles ahead of us—was a muddy valley and impassable. I thought he must have been exaggerating. All around us the dryness was evident, not a drop of water, and it seemed impossible for tanks to be stuck in a muddy wadi. A few moments later he was under T-34 tank's fire. The jeeps and two AMX tanks were stuck, and the jeeps fired on the attacking tanks and their crews. On several occasions we had jeep-to-tank battle, and Arie silenced the tanks and pulled out of the wadi. We had to choose a different route to advance south toward Nahel, and while studying the maps the first Katiusha shells hit the area around us. We were fully exposed. A large concentration of forces was in an open field and in range. Again the state of danger was stripped of reality for me. We were on the jeep, the shells raised dust and smoke as they fell, but not for a moment did I have the feeling that anything might really happen. We discovered the Abirik locality to be empty and could see enemy tanks on the slopes. Their fire was soon silenced, and Itzik went to an observation point when one of our self-propelled gun crews was suddenly under fire. This was one of the very few cases when our own forces mistook us for the enemy and fortunately Itzik noticed the mistake in time. We didn't return fire and emergency net was put in operation to communicate with the firing battalion—of another Israeli division heading west—and stop it. Considering the fact that the enemy is often equipped with identical weapons, the lack of observation aircraft or helicopters attached permanently to each force, and the long ranges, it is amazing and remarkable that mistakes occurred so seldom. Meanwhile, Arie and his reconnaissance advanced toward a burned-out radar post on top of a hill to check on a new axis and Dov suggested we drive there. We drove fast and overtook Arie's half-track. He stopped and was a bit annoyed with the "people from headquarters" getting in front of him. He ordered us to follow behind his force. Just below the radar Arie opened fire on escaping crews of an armored personnel carrier and destroyed an armored vehicle which was burning when we reached it a few moments later. Glued to the hill above it were about sixty corpses. Little spots of khaki flew up as they tried to run and hide. The flames generated heat as far as the road and we drove up to a ridge where Arie dispersed his tanks and jeeps observing the track below.

This was it now. We were to chase and destroy. The task was no more a political or strategic advantage, in the global sense of "reaching the Canal," or "opening the blockade," or even "hitting at the core." This was done in Um-Katef and other forces were enabled to run forward. Now we were to destroy enemy forces wherever they were—another carrier, another tank, another company. An unpleasant task, perhaps, but a preventive one. Eleven years ago we were in this area and the enemy was defeated rather than fully destroyed. This time we had to assure maximal destruction.

We were out of cigarettes. The four of us on the jeep were smokers and we stopped at a turned-over truck. Katz and Itzik went to search the front cabin for cigarettes while we were watching and covering them. A few kit bags were thrown next to some heavy shoes and they turned them upside down—no luck. Out of the kit bags fell uniforms, underwear, a new pair of shoes, some writing paper, a beret, a battle dress, socks. The truck was loaded with blankets, boxes of ammunition, some suitcases, no cigarettes. Some soldiers in an observation point, who didn't notice Dov's field ranks, shouted at us that looting was forbidden. We drove over to Arie. He was watching the enormous plain confronting him. He was out of fuel, he said. Dov said we were going to the radar post. "You can't. I haven't cleared it yet, there may be armed men in the tents and bunkers."

When Arie realized we were going anyway he sent a command car with armed men along with us. We cocked the guns. I was loading mine, not taking it too seriously, and the sight that met us was an unpleasant one. Next to the radar and an antiaircraft gun a few corpses lay folded. The radar site had been hit by an air attack and burned, and the corpses were scorched to the bone. Itzik and Katz shot a few rounds at tent entrances "to try the guns." I guess their fingers were burning, just to touch the trigger, not to kill or destroy but to fire, to belong. More shoes, new pairs of socks, no cigarettes.

We drove down and back to the division. Between the radar site and the headquarters half-tracks there were a few tents, fenced and unhurt. We parked the jeep and walked in. This must have been officers' quarters and the treasures were numerous. We did find some cigarettes, a better brand named Cleopatra, and some matches. Neatly pressed suits of uniforms hung in a field cupboard and suitcases displayed a variety of objects. There were blue and yellow physical-training outfits, civilian dacron sports shirts, pajamas, and clean underwear. What the corpses didn't make real for me, this room did. Suddenly the enemy became a human entity. He preferred green to blue, he had a gold watch and a wedding ring which—leaving in haste—he didn't bother to take. He was size 42 jacket and his shoes were of suede. His roommate read comics and thrillers, he had a pretty dark-haired wife and two children the photo of whom was in a drawer. We opened a bedside cupboard. Out fell a dozen pairs of black nylon stockings made in East Germany. Six Revlon eye-liner sets, cheap perfume, some other cosmetics. We laughed. But it was a real person who stocked those goods. Did he keep them as gifts for wives, or were they given to female visitors? Itzik and Katz were slightly bewildered. The insignia on the shirts proved the occupants to be officers. One was a doctor. A few books on general medicine, some photographs. Dov went out. "That will do," he said. "Do you need anything?" we asked. "Tooth paste and shaving cream," he joked back. An additional search produced what he wanted. The products were called Castella. I took a mirror with painted birds and flowers on its back—made in China, a box of chocolate candies, a macintosh, a dozen pencils, made in China again, and some writing paper and envelopes. I felt tired. The laughter at the finds turned to disgust and contempt. I knew what our officers' bedside tables contained. An Egyptian soldier would have found a few pens, writing paper, a few books and study matter—perhaps a book of poems, some photographs, a simple shaving kit, letters from home. The tenants here must have joined the retreating division from Kseime—if they hadn't escaped earlier—and were now on their way to the Canal to be destroyed by our air force or advanced forces. Arik met us with, "Where on earth were you?" It was past lunchtime and we had been gone for a couple of hours. I made a light lunch. Other parts of the division were arriving in the assembly zone. We were promised water and were waiting for the cargo to be dropped before we could continue. An area was marked for the dropping, and Arik drove to the tents we came from. We followed him and circled the camp when Dov stopped the jeep and jumped out. "Look what I found!" Well camouflaged and dug in was a brand-new amphibious Russian tank, large and yellow and unused. While we were trying to open a screw on it, Sason, the Shermans' commander, showed up with a few tankists. In five minutes they were in it traversing its gun. Seconds later the engine was started, and grinning Sason drove it out, maneuvering it toward his battalion in a cloud of happy dust, saluting Arik on the way.

The Nords appeared in the sky. Red and yellow smoke grenades were thrown as indicators and the enormous white parachutes filled the sky. It was a happy sight. Somehow I never quite believed that those things worked. Supply, ammunition, and water followed us along the way. I always regarded as miraculous their arrival when needed. The large crates contained plastic jericans of water and it was hard work preventing the soldiers from taking the parachutes and turning them into souvenir scarves and shirts.

A large helicopter landed, bringing papers and blank postcards. I shall never forget the sight of tired troops dashing and besieging the helicopter, snatching the papers and reading them hungrily, filling in the cards, scribbling an address in haste so the pilot could take them back and mail them to the rear. Most of them wrote just one line—"I am well, we are winning all along." Reservists added kisses to the children. The helicopter was about to take off and soldiers were still streaming toward it, the pilot bending down to take more postcards. He must have carried with him more than a thousand that day. A thousand hopeful faces followed it in its flight, a thousand homes would read the one or two lines a couple of days later with relief.

I looked at the newspaper. Headlines declared: "The Gaza Strip is in our hands, the army is taking over cities in the west bank." "Ramallah is ours." There were greetings from factories, farms, schools—wishing their reservists a fast victory and a safe return.

"Soft drinks Tempo" factory, "The Oil Refineries," "Ort Schools," "Port Authority," "Crystal mixers and washing machines" plants were all telling their drafted workers "We are with you—wherever you are." Next to those a large announcement by the American Embassy advising all American citizens to leave Israel, and then, in the inside page—the first horrible sight of names in black frames—"Captain Yoram Harpaz fell fulfilling his duty." "Lieutenant Amiram Manor was killed in action." "Our beloved Uri . . ."

My first tears. I didn't know Yoram or Amiram or Uri. I knew other Yorams and Uris who were now in uniform, and those were only the first ones. Opposite me, asleep under half-tracks or lunching near the jeeps, were other Yorams and Amirams, and they were sons of mothers who shivered every time there was a knock on the door. We were between Um-Katef and Nahel, we were victorious, we were winning on three fronts, but at that moment even those three first names I saw were worth more than that. I saw a soldier looking at my paper behind my back. Did he imagine his own name framed in black? Did he know Amiram or Uri? Something saddened his face and he turned to walk away. I wasn't left with time to ponder. At four o'clock Arik said we were moving and the long trip south recommenced. The axis we took was the roughest road I've ever been on. The forces moved with the frustration of withheld slow motion—another 100 yards, another mile—the ground was broken, wadi beds, heaps of hard clay forming a labyrinth of artistic shapes turning each mile into five miles—not much improved by the fact that the tanks softened it up. Dov tried to by-pass but we were stuck in a worse wadi and had to return. On the horizon we could see a mountain silhouetted against an evening sky. A beautiful sunset and then darkness. We continued to drive as if in a dream —automatically holding to the wheel, to the machine gun, to the road.

It grew cooler; a wind was blowing; we were hungry and exhausted, and the road stretched forward lit by hundreds of headlights. A troop carrier was destroyed on the way and, burning, acted as a signal to the caravan. Like a giant torch it threw light and warmth on the passing tanks and cars as if checking them out to a cooler and a darker unknown.

I had lost sense of time. I knew our whereabouts by looking at the map, but futility infiltrated. It all seemed endless. I covered myself with a blanket as well as the pullover and jacket. Dov had to admit it was cold and put on a windbreaker and we drove parallel to Arik's half-track when the convoy stopped. It was almost midnight. We continued to drive to the head of the convoy to see what happened. We left behind us the armored battalions and reached their reconnaissance patrol. They were on top of a hill on the verge of a plateau and were dispersed in a formation in a line vertical to the convoy. We drove in a circle to look for the commander when we heard his voice. "Don't move! You are in a middle of a minefield." His tone was nervous. He obviously considered us superfluous in a minefield. Dov was dubious about the statement. "You think so?" he asked. "Yes, and the convoy must stop until the engineers have cleared a route through it." It was a clear night. The jeeps were frozen in place and the men didn't budge. Ahead of us a few empty crates were scattered. "Nobody is as stupid as to leave mine crates behind to mark a minefield." "They were in a hurry. You'd better follow your own tracks going back."

We didn't. Again the proximity of danger didn't register

and between the warning and reality lay the cool night air, the starry sky, the safe sight of the convoy, soft sound of singing voices.

We drove back to join Arik. Motke's half-track was next to his. Arik was listening to the net. He looked at us and said, "A jeep was just blown up on a mine. Two soldiers were killed." I don't think we dared tell him we'd just been there. A few minutes later we heard the sentence which shook us all. "The Old City of Jerusalem is ours."

Did I say fatigue? Minefield, late night, middle of the Sinai—it all disappeared. Suddenly there was the Temple Mount and the Wailing Wall and the heart too small to contain those words. Was it joy that brought tears to the toughest soldiers? Pride? Sense of history or religion? All I know is that the news was cried out and the convoy was lit as if by lightning. The "something" had happened. It was not a conquest but liberation, it was not our long route to Nahel, it was the long route of our people, from Moses to the paratrooper who first touched the sacred wall. We were suddenly not defending a frontier, a settlement, a decade, we were a part of something that was larger. The existence and dreams and hopes and future of a people—in New York and Moscow and Um-Katef and Rio-de-Janeiro. The religious ones were praying, the others, whispering a song which became the anthem of the War—Naomi Shemer's "Jerusalem of Gold"—a song written shortly before the war, mourning the "City with a Wall in Its Heart."

Now the wall was in our hearts and the city united and David in the Centurion, Zeeb in the "Bell," Tzipi in the rear headquarters, Katz in the jeep, the mothers of Uri and Amiram and Yoram—they were all walking by the wall, they engulfed the Tower of David and gazed down from Mount Scopus. We were a few miles from Nahel, isolated by mines. Our supply echelons were stuck along the road in the rough broken ground, but the sense of solitude was gone. We were all in the market place of the Old City, on the road to Jericho, with Solomon and David and our ancestors.

"We'd better get a few hours' sleep while we can," Arik suggested, and we all crowded between the two half-tracks. Motke joined us, and I asked Arik, "Can you manage a meal or would you rather sleep?" "Never refuse food," he said. In a few moments the tea was ready and I heated some meat. I mixed it with canned vegetables and the taste was improved. Sharm-El Sheikh was in our hands. That's where it all started, perhaps, the blockade ended and the Egyptians defeated, but somehow the news of Jerusalem was above all other victories. Dov produced the leftover of our whisky—the right time and place—and we drank "Lechaim" to our new-old capital. The box of chocolates kindly left us by an unknown Egyptian completed the celebration. Three minutes later we were all asleep, crowded in the narrow space between the half-tracks. With dawn, a route was cleared in the minefield and we resumed our advance. Motke's brigade was leading—split along three routes—and we, in the jeep, hopped from one to another. From a top of a hill we could see the convoy. We were near Nahel now and the vehicles moved rather fast. A long snake of khaki and dust, a huge animal crawling tailless as far as the eye could see. When the convoy stopped, we drove down for breakfast. Dayan's words in the Old City were broadcast again: "We have united Jerusalem, the divided capital of Israel—we have returned to the holiest of our holy places, never to part from it again." These were words of vow. "Never again," "forever." We believed in them.

THURSDAY, JUNE 8

I climbed the half-track with plates and cups and a teakettle. Arik was having breakfast on the map on top of his command half-track. Shaike, general commanding south, was telling him on the radio that an Egyptian armored brigade was seen from the air on the move from Kuntila and Temed on its way to help 4th Tank Division under attack around Bir-Gafgafa. The Bell helicopter just arrived from the rear with Zeev at its controls. Itzik was despatched to have a look on the road, some ten miles south. He reported hundreds of vehicles and tens of tanks and guns on the road between Temed and Nahel. In a matter of minutes Arik, while eating his breakfast, decided on the plan for ambush and attack. We didn't know at that time the mood of the enemy. Was he running away, was he on the way to the second line of defense to join the 4th Division, was he on an orderly retreat? And who exactly was he? What could we expect from· the units we were going to encounter? We knew that in Temed and Kuntila the Egyptians had quite some forces, lured there by the maneuvers of our forces. We knew that in this area Brig. Shazly was blowing up a lot of air and clouds of dust. Shazly was everywhere according to reports. He made quite a fuss with himself and his "Special Shazly Force." Colonel Dan Hiram, who was our military attaché in London, knew Shazly well and met him for several clandestine talks while he was Egyptian military attaché, and many others knew him when he was a battalion commander of the Egyptian contingent in the Congo, in Lumumba's days. Dov remembered reading the *Diplomatist,* a prestige paper catering to the vanity of the diplomatic colony in London, where Shazly proclaimed himself an expert on military science and strategy. The boys were anxious to meet the fellow in the field and teach him a lesson or two in strategy. But he was nowhere to be found. He must have "carried out a strategical withdrawal" quite early.

We didn't know how many troops were pulled out from Temed during the two last nights but we supposed that a great part of the 6th Division should be there. This means we may meet with the 1st Armored Brigade, the 8th, and maybe the 13th Infantry Brigades, and many other support units, artillery etc.

Earlier in the morning a force from an armored brigade that was left in defense against Kuntila was put under Arik's command. They had armor and a battalion of infantry. Now their second-in-command was on our radio net telling Arik that he was pressing forward through Kuntila, which he found deserted, toward Nahel. He was ordered by Arik to pursue the retreating enemy and to join us as soon as possible. Prisoners he took told him that the Egyptians were going to defend Temed, a locality to the southeast of Nahel, which offered many advantages for the defender. A passing Piper Cub dropped him a note that "the enemy is digging in Temed." He, later to be known to us as the "Mustached Motke," put his whole force in high gear and was chasing full speed after the enemy, not giving him time to defend the high ground of Temed. They caught up with some fifteen T-34 tanks, destroyed two, and from all the others the crews just jumped out and ran away. At two in the afternoon the force got into Temed, but found not a soul. Later in the evening, when he met us at Nahel, he claimed between forty to sixty enemy tanks to his unit's credit. He may have claimed some that were destroyed by the air force, but nobody cared. This will be the job of logistic command and their staff of operations research whiz kids to establish exactly what should be credited to whose conduct sheet.

The Nahel Ambush

Nahel is a godforsaken place in spite of the fact that it has plenty of water. You should have tasted the water! It was smelly, sickly sweet, and greasy. Arik and Dov knew Nahel by heart from last time. A few houses, an army camp, a hill or two overlooking them and the road to the Mitla Pass, and the Canal doing a 90 degree bend. Last time we took it in matter of minutes, had some canned bully beef, and sped to the Mitla.

How will it be this time? Motke got his orders through Itzik, who came by helicopter. His Centurions were sent earlier to the aid of Iska's brigade of Jaffe's division, they shouldn't be too far away. "Call them back and place them in ambush southwest of the road a mile or two outside Nahel." The Shermans were a mile ahead of us; they should wait just outside west of Nahel on both sides of the road. Hertzel with his infantry in half-tracks would hit the rear of the Egyptian column, coming out into the plain from behind Nahel ridge. Motke got the helicopter for a few minutes, had a look at the convoy, and was quite pleased with what he saw. "Open fire only from 200 yards," was the order. Sason was moving in full speed because the observation post on the hill reported the enemy tanks pressing toward Nahel. In the very first minutes of encounter his men knocked out seven to nine tanks. Some of the tanks were changing direction, leaving the road and heading for the village and Nahel army camp. Sason was in a jeep and his N Company followed him to destroy three or five more tanks. Minutes later the Centurions arrived and hit the convoy a mile farther. Arik took Hertzel and his half-tracks to the rear and east of Nahel. His own half-track broke down so he abandoned it and jumped into our jeep. We were running like mad in the dust to an observation post on the edges of Nahel ridge. Suddenly over our radio we were told the air force was going to give us support. We stopped the jeep on the slope and climbed up the side, the profile, of the hill. We saw Egyptian Centurion tanks, six of them, on the road. They looked massive and well protected among many more vehicles. It would be silly to expose oneself in half-tracks or jeeps to the guns of these behemoths of Centurions. Arik was given by Motke, the night before, a sickly Centurion of our own as his personal anti-tank bodyguard. This became useful now. Hertzel got the Centurion from Arik as it and the anti-tank weapon followed him behind his jeep.

The air force appeared in the blue sky. Four super-Mystere's came in low strafing and pouring napalm on the tanks. We all got very excited, Dov standing and calmly taking in the whole

84

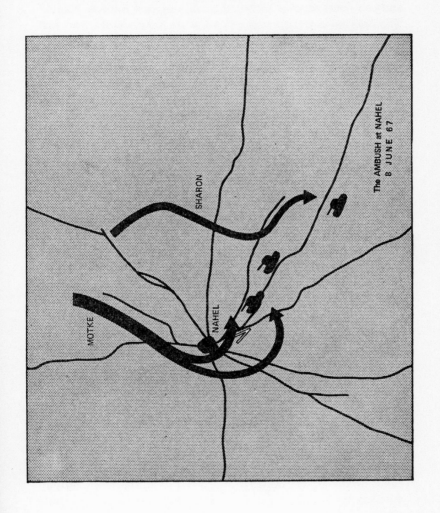

The AMBUSH at NAHEL
8 JUNE 67

scene on his 8-mm. Canon Cine camera "just like on maneuvers."

The planes dived two or three times. I hoped they recognized us. Their hits were too precise to risk not being identified. We were too near their targets. On their fourth circle they waved shalom to us, tilting their wings. A few days later I met one of the pilots—Arik, a classmate of mine from Nahalal. "I always knew we'd operate together one day," he said. They flew northeast, and we jumped into our jeep and sped to the road below. We got dangerously close to the burning tanks; ammunition was exploding in all directions. We were ordered by Arik to go back. He himself got into another jeep. He was trying to spare me the sight of the chase, the hunt for the remnants of the enemy. Dov wasn't very happy to go all the way back and suggested to Arik we should go along with the armored infantry, on the road to Nahel. Arik was weighing what was the greater risk. Suddenly there was fire behind us. Some of our men were exchanging small-arms fire with Egyptian soldiers hiding in a bush a few yards away. We must have been lucky, because only ten minutes earlier we had passed the same bushes raising a protective cloud of dust. We were allowed to follow the armored infantry on their mopping-up way into Nahel. Half-tracks, Russian jeeps, tanks were burning and smoking all over the place; guns, armored personnel carriers were thrown in all directions and positions. Hundreds of Egyptian soldiers were running away in the direction of Nahel. Later they told us they thought the place was still theirs. Our soldiers were calling for them to surrender. Some did, others answered with a shot or a burst or ran away. In front of me I saw a young soldier from one of our half-tracks shoot an Egyptian, run behind the armored car, put his arm against the backboard, and vomit, then instantly compose himself and catch up with his section.

I was holding a Uzi submachine gun, Dov was driving, Katz was at the front machine gun, and Itzik was pointing a Russian automatic gun. None of us fired. Others were doing the job and we were watching. Corpses lined our way. We went down to pick up their guns, those hiding in bushes engaging us were shot at and groups were running away in all directions. Those who stopped to aim were killed. Some escaped, but I couldn't free myself from the feeling that it was a hunt rather than a fight. I was not going to shoot. The men in the jeep were armed and if we were shot at directly they could return fire. Yet, my gun was loaded and cocked. My face was burning—the skin tight with dust and sweat which turned into mud. My sunglasses were useless, and in my eyes there was a stinging pain. Added to the midday heat was the heat of the burning vehicles, a miniature inferno, hateful and ugly.

We came into Nahel late in the afternoon. There we met more destruction, wholesale as only tanks can do to tanks. This was the Valley of Death of the Egyptian army. About one hundred and fifty tanks were counted on the road from Temed to Nahel. Nobody counted the vehicles, the guns, the big heavy ones, the small anti-tank, the light antiaircraft, the heavy tractors towing the guns, the big ammunition trucks all in unnatural positions, or in piles, looking like pieces of modern sculpture.

The sight was depressing and Dov was very silent at the wheel. Later that evening, while we were having tea, he told me he was almost crying for the fate of these Egyptian soldiers. "What a miserable fate they had depending on such bastard leaders and officers. In 1948, they had the pashas and their incompetent sons as officers; in 1956, in the Sinai, you could excuse them somehow—they weren't yet educated and prepared, the socialist revolution hadn't yet had enough time to close the gap between officer and his men. But now, sixteen years after the revolution, with officers trained in Russia, with Russian experts in Egypt, where is the spirit of socialism? How come we had only one or two officers prisoners and countless soldiers? How come we didn't take or see one staff car? Where were all the laughing officers in their glittering

uniforms and wavy hair smothered with brillantine, so con-
fident-looking on Cairo television and in the pages of the illus-
trated papers? The poor felaheen were abandoned to their
fate, to the mercy of our troops, the enemy. How could he,
Nasser, whom I considered to be an honest leader of his nation, play with the lives of his people, bluff at the expense
of these thousands and thousands of obedient sons of Egypt,
how could he play high politics, putting them as a pawn in
the game? He was in no position to play Napoleon to close
the straits of Tiran, to threaten us with a thousand tanks in
Sinai and arrogantly to invite General Rabin, for what? He had
more pressing problems to solve than prestige. He didn't have
enough to feed his population but spent billions on arms, his
people were illiterate. Why the hell did he start all this when
he used to tell the world he wasn't ready yet? Why didn't he
let us and his own people live in peace?" I let him talk, half-
listening. Some needed silence, others needed words. Arik, the
legendary fighter, let a mist of gray cover his face. "It is horrible," he said, "I hate it," and found escape in a couple of
hours' sleep on a camp bed under a tent erected between two
half-tracks. He asked Dov to look for a better place for headquarters. We were surrounded by corpses where we were and
we drove to look for a relatively clear site. I didn't believe my
skin would ever regain its natural softness. "Don't put water on
it," someone said. "What happened to you?" I was asked. I
dared look in the mirror—finding a shelter in a cabin of a jeep
from the sandstorm that swept through the camp. It was not
my face that I saw. My eyes were red, humid pools in the
middle of a yellow deadly tight-skinned image. I rubbed
cream on my cheeks. The skin peeled off in large swatches. It
changed colour from yellow to red to brown patches—I didn't
care. I knew nothing would be the same now. I had looked at
cessation of life, destruction of matter, sorrow of destroyers,
agony of the victorious, and it had to leave a mark. The Syrians continued to shell our settlements—Tel Katzir, Haon,
Hulata, Gonen, Shamir—places I knew well, populated by

classmates, friends from the scouts' movement, acquaintances, relatives. The war was still on there; in some places it hadn't yet begun, but for us in Nahel it was over. The aftermath of battle, the results of war, the total fatigue were evident, and we were to live with them for a while, but the actual fighting in the Sinai was over, we had won our battle. Now we had to live with the victory. It was almost dark, and the few buildings of Nahel were silhouetted against the desert backdrop. The sandstorm receded, and silence took over. The horn of a burning vehicle was operating—a wan sound of alarm not to die for hours—like a soft reminder of what was.

During the Sinai Campaign Dov and Arik found a stock of bully beef in Nahel. While approaching it, Arik expressed the hope that it was still there and we vaguely were looking for it. I don't know of a place uglier than Nahel. The wilderness of Paran. Here Hagar dwelt with her son exiled by Abraham. It is supposed to be an oasis, and a few trees indicate the presence of water. We soon found the well and filled up containers after the doctors had examined the water. If we drank the water, it was for lack of any other for the taste was abominable. We drove toward the group of buildings—rather new constructions, some only half-finished—and looked for beef cans and a site clean of corpses to move the headquarters to. A small house painted white and blue had a neat feeling about it, and Dov entered. Through the window I could see an iron bed and a corpse on it. In front of another house a pile of watermelons was prey for flies—the first watermelons I'd seen this season, and the local bakery had trays of wood with dry dough formed into pita-bread shape set to be baked.

The flies, the dirt, and the dead were everywhere, and the purity of desert air, the absence of objects and smells and colors, was gone. Instructions concerning loot were very strict and only brigade commanders were allowed to add to the brigade supplies local goods found in a few abandoned stores. It was dark now, a moonless night, and we returned to the half-track. I prepared some food—it was the end of our K-rations and the supply convoy was delayed on the axis we had left in worse shape than it originally was. I don't remember a sadder evening. Very few words were spoken, but we shared the depression and avoided looking at one another. A great part of it was owing to fatigue, and although a commanders' meeting was to take place in the half tent where the beds were, I covered myself with a blanket and fell asleep.

FRIDAY, JUNE 9

Friday morning found me surprised by the fact I was asleep on a bed. It took me a minute to realize where I was. Arik was asleep on the second bed, Dov between us on two benches, and the helicopter pilot who by now, unshaved and dirty, looked like a regular infantryman, on the ground next to my bed. "We've got to move from here," Arik said, and indicated the visible fact that we were surrounded by corpses.

A suitable place was found a mile or so away, exposed to sandstorms and as unappealing as the rest of the "oasis" but it did seem cleaner and it was time to get organized. The trailer arrived from Shivta, shaken and filthy, and we spent an hour while Arik was on tour to wash and clean it. A couple of tents were erected and an Indian tent for the kitchen. Rachamim was grinning. "I really couldn't work under field conditions, on the move," he admitted. "Now we can cook!" Two pup tents were our provisory homes and a barbed-wire fence was erected around the headquarters site. The rear headquarters arrived as well and undertook the burden of administrative, personnel, and logistic problems. Colonel Uri, with the battalions from Kseime, joined us.

Arik issued disciplinary orders. The men were to shave and wash and field showers were erected. The water was good enough for washing if for nothing else, and the post-battle anticlimax had to be met by imposing order and a field routine.

Operational activity continued. Patrols circulated in the area returning with more prisoners, and the Temed–Nahel road was still an unsafe axis. Egyptian soldiers who fled during the battles were searching for water and food, and their sources were the well-guarded well in Nahel and the radiators of destroyed vehicles along the road. Some surrendered themselves asking for water as they did so, but many were still carrying guns and constituted a danger. Toward lunchtime a patrol returned and arrived at headquarters with a stretcher covered with a blanket. They had been patrolling the road when out of one of the tanks a few soldiers emerged. They raised up their hands, there were seven of them, confronting three of ours. Our soldiers by now didn't expect resistance and while they were approaching, one of the Egyptians fired—one of our men died instantly, the others took revenge, soon enough, but they brought the dead with a feeling that his death was not inevitable. The first helicopter evacuated him and patrols yielded to stricter rules.

I went to see the prisoners. They were sitting on the ground, shoeless and bareheaded, and a few of them were slightly wounded. A group of soldiers surrounded them staring, and after the patrol's incident some were teasing them. Arik instructed them to be moved to a site next to ours and forbade our soldiers to approach them. Zeevale and I checked with them again later in the day. They were now given blankets and hats and sufficient drinking water. There were about seventy of them and new ones arrived on the hour. They ate the same K-rations we were given and to judge by their faces, they had never had better food. We talked to our armored brigade doctor and he said he could treat the wounded and sent an ambulance to fetch them.

I asked the guard, who spoke Arabic, whether any of the prisoners spoke English and he introduced me to George.

George was a man in his thirties. Profession—a physician. His slacks were torn and he wore a blanket around his midriff; an arm band indicated his profession. Zeevale offered him a cigarette and we sat apart from the others chatting. When the convoy was attacked, he remembered, he was in his hospital car but abandoned it. He fled to a nearby hill and watched the battle. When it was over, he walked a few miles raising his hands until he met an Israeli patrol and was brought here. He knew Jews in Cairo and didn't mind his present position. Complaints? He would have liked to be able to treat the wounded among the prisoners. There was dysentry and he wanted a supply of tablets. He also wanted to be able to assure the other prisoners—he was a major—that they were not going to be maltreated or killed. Zeevale smiled. His smile was boyish, a Nahalal boy. You can certainly assure them, he said. We explained to him that we ourselves had shortage of water. George said the food was good and in quantity. His wife of one year was pregnant. "That's the only thing that makes me want to go back." The ambulance arrived and George pointed out the wounded. Three of them had fragments in hands and legs, by now infected. Two who suggested they were wounded were dismissed by George as "not serious," but our doctor took them anyway. One had a head wound and had to stay in hospital. George was promised tablets and disinfectants as many of them had lice. "Tell me," Zeevale asked him. "Why did they run away? Why did tank crews desert their tanks? Why didn't they use their arms?" "They were astonished," George replied. "We didn't expect it to happen like this. Radio announcements told us of victory and we knew you to be inferior. The officers ran away a day earlier and confusion set in." He kept murmuring—"We were astonished." We left them to go back—a small barbed-in group of pathetic creatures, happy to remain alive, frightened and prideless, squatting and clutching a water can, awaiting their fate.

Something was going to happen in Syria, we knew or rather

sensed. The Sinai was ours and the west bank of the Jordan was in Israeli hands. The Syrians were shelling our settlements and we didn't think this was the end of the war. Our officers were restless. Uri, whose home village was not far from the Syrian border, asked permission to go north. "My men will be all right here. I have to go, up north is my war, and I've got to be there. Here our job is done." Arik consented halfheartedly, leaving the final decision to Uri. Somewhere, half-admittedly, he, too, would have liked to be transferred north where a job still had to be done. Egypt and Jordan accepted a cease fire, Syria did not, and if a couple of days earlier soldiers and officers had said, "I wish I were in Jerusalem," now they were saying, "I wish I could be sent to Syria." Fighting in Syria, more than on other fronts, meant the protection of settlements permanently exposed to fire and infiltrators.

A helicopter landed in the early evening with the most precious of loads—mail and newspapers. Reading the paper, Friday the ninth, felt like reading science fiction. Somehow we were unable to digest the news items.

Zim, the Israeli navigation company, announces it reopens its Eilat–East Africa Line. Egged, the bus company, renews No. 9 bus to Mount Scopus after ninteen years. The driver of the first bus is the son of a bus driver killed in 1948 on the same route.

Kibbutz Nahal-Oz, on the Egyptian frontier, for years battling infiltrators and fire, thanks the army for placing them in the rear. Soviet Russia demands a general and total retreat, and the Israeli air force is attacking targets in Syria. Zubin Mehta, the Indian conductor, will conduct the Israeli Philharmonic in a "victory concert" on Mount Scopus. A list of movies, a list of contributors to the emergency fund, Ben Gurion's visit to the Wailing Wall—"This is the second great day in my life. The first was when I immigrated to Israel." Helicopters rescuing jet pilots, greetings to the army from plants, farm settlements, and factories. Kibbutz Haon greets its soldiers but adds—"The parents are worried, please write, at home all is well," and the first poems of war:

> *"The regiment marches to target*
> *and the rear sends it a 'shalom,'*
> *Words like 'freedom' and 'homeland'*
> *never cease to be reborn."*
>
> —GAMZU

But life goes on, and the movie critic writes a review, art exhibitions in the galleries, an article on Pasternak. The evening sandstorm made reading difficult and I watched with jealousy those who received letters. Their faces were relaxed, smiling, a tear in eyes. They were in another world, the baby was gaining weight, little Ruthy sent a drawing, the girl friend writes, "I know you'll win and be back, but take care." A mother worries about the cold and shortage of water. A friend from another front describes the prewar days. Never were letters reread so often, folded like treasures and placed so carefully in the shirt pocket close to the heart.

Arik was preparing for an evening officers' meeting and I got permission to use the jeep and visit one of the units. Katz went along, and we were stopped twice for the password which we didn't know. We arrived at a small forest where the reconnaissance patrol men were sitting around a bonfire. When they had brought the dead that morning they told me they'd got some coffee and here it was, in a large can, sending waves of missed aroma. Coffee was not included in the rations and we had been drinking tea, which is a drink better suited to desert heat. Still, the coffee now added to the end-of-war feeling and we chatted for a couple of hours. The argument was a simple one—is the Egyptian soldier basically bad, or is it his officer, his training, his background? "Give Arik a division of Arab soldiers, and let him keep his own officers—they will be as good fighters as we are," was one opinion. The others claimed that "even if I never had training, and faced a

95

fierce enemy, and had no commander, I'd fight the same way I do now. With less skill, perhaps, but as much devotion." They were quite shocked and almost moved by the cowardice they had met in the enemy. "If you knew you were bound to lose and be killed, would you still fight?" I asked. Some said yes, others said they would surrender but behave differently when prisoners. I felt as though I were watching a trial, judging the qualities of the enemy, and I had to half-smile when it was obvious that these boys almost wished they had a better enemy, of a quality they could understand. While we were talking a shot was fired in our direction. The bullet whistled above our heads and was lost in the dark. "Put off the fire," the captain said and sent four soldiers to search in the direction from which the shot was fired. It was late and they, too, were tired, and a few moments later we parted. Driving through the sleeping camp, I thought how exposed our concentration was.

The officers' meeting was just over and Motke asked me to join the armor officers the following evening for dinner. Someone said, "Shabat shalom," reminding us it was Friday night. A week earlier I was at home packing, an eternity ago.

The Days After

On Saturday the battle with Syria continued. Friday night the outposts on the slopes were taken after hard battles, and Saturday our forces were advancing to Kuneitra on the road to Damascus. With the frustration of "we should have been in Cairo now" soldiers hoped our forces would enter Damascus. The radio announced "our forces are along the line Mas'ada–Kuneitra–Butmiya, some 20 kilometers east of the frontier. The removal of the Syrians east of this line prevents them from shelling villages in Israel."

This meant no Israeli settlement was now within range of an Arab enemy. Excluding the Lebanese–Israeli frontier. We were out of K-rations and I was promised supplies by lunchtime when Dov surprised me with the "gift of the war." We are going for a drive, he said. I mounted the jeep, as he suggested—took a towel and a change of clothes. "Are we going for a swim in the Suez?" I asked. Not quite. He drove a few miles behind low hills and produced from the back of the car a jerican of water. "Here, you can shower." He turned away from me to watch and inspect underground ammunition stores that we saw on our way here, and I improvised a shower by, once undressed, propping the container tilted so as to have a steady flow of water. It was a strange sight, a naked woman in the middle of the Sinai; saving on water but making sure the soap and fluid reached every bit of skin. I realized how filthy the clothes were. The sun had turned my fore-arms, face, and neck black, leaving the rest of the body pale and sickly. "You'd better hurry," Dov said. On the slopes in the distance our patrols were looking for thirsty prisoners and no site really felt empty and isolated. Every bush could hide a hungry Egyptian, every trench a corpse. I put on clean clothes—a very becoming thing to do on Saturday. Dov said, "To quote your uncle Eizer (Gen. Eizer Weitzman), who was quoting an English lady: 'When an Arab is dirty, he's pictur-esque, but when a Jew is dirty, he's a dirty Jew.' So better try to stay clean now."

I couldn't believe my eyes when we returned and entered the kitchen tent. Not only had we received K-rations but a great variety of fresh supplies. I couldn't resist the bread and cut a slice. The taste of bread after a week of hard crackers! I also ran out of improvizations on K-rations. A box of rations enabled me to make meat with peas, peas with corn, corn with meat, meat with corn and peas, beans with any of the above, fried sausage meat, sardines with cucumbers, sardines with olives, and cucumbers, and all those were done and served—hot and cold—always extracting from Arik an ex-clamation and a compliment. "How did you cook this wonder-ful stew?" he would ask facing again the meat-peas-and-corn combination heated in the empty chocolate box. Now I felt queenly. Eggs, tomato, onion, green peppers, fresh rations —by now a different variety, as the army had run out on the supplies, and food factories threw in new types of canned food—and bread. With sunset I went to Motke's trailer, mean-ing to be back in time to cook a good and different dinner.

When I entered the armored brigade camp it was with a feeling of a return to a familiar site. Tolstoi's *War and Peace* came alive, books on nineteenth-century battles, Russian ar-mies in fields of snow. Groups of people cuddled around bon-fires, and singing was heard, nostalgic and moving from be-hind tanks and half-tracks. Soldiers were asleep under blan-kets, while others served food in mess tins, and through the

98

thin clouds emerged a new baby moon, thin like a razor's edge, perfect and hopeful.

Motke took me to a large tent where his officers were assembled. On camp beds salad was served in helmets and slices of bread were passed. A supply of cold soft drinks arrived, and chocolate-coated biscuits found in an Egyptian store added to the feast. A bottle of cognac changed hands. I was seated between Sason and Motke. Motke got up to speak. He did not mourn the dead, he praised the living. He counted acts of heroism—wounded tankists refusing to leave their tanks, soldiers taking command once a commander was killed, tanks breaking through minefields to open the route for the others. He talked about Jerusalem, about Gaza and the Canal, the Syrian heights. He thanked his rear echelons, the cooks and the mechanics, the drivers and the morale officers. "Let's sing now!" he said, and in an unexpectedly beautiful voice started singing the hymn of the armored brigades. Other songs followed—the songs of the war. As if nothing happened in between, soldiers sang the 1948 songs and the 1956 ones. Revived were Palmach songs and Sinai songs and added to them "Jerusalem of Gold," and this week's songs, already popular—a song to the Daughter Michal, a love song to the White Desert, a letter home, at home all is well. All the songs mentioned home, most of them were sentimental, all of them were written with love—to the light of Jerusalem, the whiteness of the Sinai, the snows of Mount Chermon, and the heights of Golan. Dov came to fetch me and back in the tent I could enjoy preparing dinner. Cutting fresh vegetables instead of opening a can seemed miraculous, the smell of eggs being fried, coffee, meat with white beans. I cooked for ten. We were only five but the food disappeared instantly. Arik suggested that Dov go north to take care of some things at the Southern command, and I decided to join him. The division was moving northwest to Bir-Gafgafa and we planned to rejoin it there three days later.

Late on Sunday morning we left Nahel. Two patrol jeeps

accompanied us part of the way. It was still unadvisable to drive alone in this area, as wandering Egyptians were likely to shoot—for water rather than patriotism. I didn't feel well. Suddenly, the wind blowing in my face was disturbing rather than pleasant, the dust became dirt, the scenery monotonous. My sunglasses didn't function well and the fatigue of a week started expressing itself. Every mile to the north meant a return to a world by now unfamiliar, and phenomena which before were tolerated with joy for a cause now had no additional dimension. We stopped in Bir-Hasana, hoping to find some water—a change from the Nahel water. There was none but we were directed to the doctors' hut and were given some distilled water from a container. Bir-Hasana boasted the largest camp of flies in the Sinai, and burned vehicles and corpses didn't exactly contribute to their extermination. The patrol left us there, and I envied them returning to the atmosphere I regarded as home. We were approaching Gebel-Libni, one of our headquarters in the Sinai. A funny feeling to knock on a door, enter a house, be met by secretaries who are clean and whose skirts are pressed. I collapsed into an armchair, was offered coffee in a real cup, sugar served in a bowl. I felt clumsy. An officer entered and looked at me. Dov was in one of the rooms expressing the needs of the division and I felt exposed. The officer grinned. "What are you looking so militant for?" Show off! I snapped. My boots were covered with layers of dust, my baggy trousers were fastened to my waist by a large belt still holding the canteen and knife. My hair was a mess, and the sleeves of my shirt cut off. I walked out and waited in the jeep. Dov understood when I said "Let's get out of here." It was my first contact with the rear, and we were still a long way away from the rear. The road from Gebel-Libni to El-Arish was a long cemetery of unburied dead. Lined along the sand-covered asphalt were hundreds of corpses. However fast we drove we couldn't escape the smell. Flesh rotting in the desert heat, reaching our nostrils through squares of cloth we tied around our faces, reaching creepily our skin and attaching itself—for good, it seemed—to the folds of our uniform, to the roots of the hair, under the nails, along the tanned exposed arms. The smells and the sights . . . folded over, legless, crushed, as if asleep peacefully, faces in the sand, faces to the sky—no painter's brush could draw the variety of positions into which had frozen those miserable soldiers. They had no identity tags, they were to have a burial where they were, and for the first time—just because I was going home to see my mother—I thought of the agony of mothers whose sons lay unidentified here, who will have to realize one day that absence means death; the agony of children who cannot even be comforted by the thought that their father died fighting for national survival, for their own protection, in their defense, courageously. Trucks and guns, and tanks, armored cars and jeeps and more tanks, an endless dead convoy of defeat. We reached El-Arish. The purifying sight of the blue of the sea—how I longed for it. The waves that wash away, the cool breeze, the wet grains of sand. "I told you you'd reach a sea," Dov said. I was grateful. We drove to the brigade commander's quarters and to my great surprise the dark smiling face of Kuti appeared. He was still holding his white stick—a map pointer, and this time, without being asked, I produced the arrowhead, as if it were a password to warriors' friendship. He showed us upstairs. Red-velvet upholstered armchairs and sofa, a glass-covered desk, a palace of Arab luxury. "My predecessor's office." He smiled. Siman-Tov brought us fried eggs and salad and Kuti described the house-to-house clearing that his brigade was engaged in here. "I have something for you," he said, and gave me a small medal in a special box. There were many in the cupboard, given as gifts to visitors. It was of metal and had an impression of the Sinai on it with the inscription "Sinai—a land of victory" in Arabic. "Most appropriate," he said, "and something for your father!" In the corner of the room a large Roman jar was covered with a blanket. "I had no time to look around yet," he apologized, "but he may like this one."

We exchanged the combat jeep with its mounted machine gun for a Lark and promised to be back in a couple of days.

We loaded the heavy jar onto the back seat and with sunset were on our way. The palm trees of El-Arish, the most beautiful dates I've ever seen, caught the sun in spiderwebs and let it slide through them. When darkness took over, we were nearing Gaza, and although we were spared the sight of bodies the smell clung to the air hopelessly. We by-passed the city of Gaza and a few moments later, suddenly, without a warning or a sign, we were back home. We had crossed the border, we had returned to Israel. The yellow and gray changed into green illuminated by the headlights of the car, and the smell of corpses which by now was a psychological leftover was overcome by the fresh, new aroma of green plants, tilled earth, cut clover, eucalyptus trees. Songs on the radio, news broadcast—Russia severed diplomatic relations with Israel, so did other Eastern countries. Security Council debate. I wasn't listening. Somehow it didn't connect. The flies of Bir-Hasana, Jud's night worrying about the infusions, the patrol's last dead, Arik's handsome face—at times worried, at times superior and happy—and diplomatic meetings in New York, in Moscow, in Washington, and Paris. "We'll return soon," I stated. "Of course," Dov said, and put his hand on mine. He must have felt the same. We drove on and just before Tel-Aviv stopped at a red traffic light. I burst into laughter. Traffic light! We were definitely back now. In the midst of square rules, speed limits, people on terraces, traffic lights, income tax, peace, the rear. And Zahala, my parents' house. Dov came in for a moment. I kissed my mother and brother and was left alone with them. My father was out, and somehow I found sufficient energy in me to make it to the hot bath and wash my hair. Above all I felt guilt. Here I was, eating eggs on toast and a roast, sleeping in my own bed, and wearing a nightgown.

In Nahel, Rachamim was cursing the wind and Arik slept

on the wooden bench. I felt guilty the minute I was clean, the food stuck in my throat, and I dreamed of infantry battles in the ditches. As early as I dared I woke up Dov. "Please let's go from here. You have to see Jerusalem first. I do, anyway." Before we left I talked to my mother and a few friends. How I feared these first talks. "Did you hear about Miriam's son?" "You didn't know Yossi was killed?" "How is Mussa?" "Didn't you know?" Did I want to know? The soldiers in the family—cousins, my brothers, relatives were all well. A good friend of mine, a reservist, was believed lost. He was a brilliant lawyer, an armor man, a neighbor in Zahala. We had campaigned together during the last elections. Fragments of memories started pushing their way up to the surface and I pushed back, locked up a door, and refused to believe. He was not gone, I decided, it was a horrible mistake, of course he'll be back.

We went to Jerusalem. A road so well known and always loved anew, a road along which I used to point out to visitors the border stones, the signs saying, Beware, frontier. This time it felt like a pilgrimage. A first trip to the united city, the city of David, Jerusalem of golden dreams now reachable. I thought of Kuti, who wanted never to find his giant white arrowhead. Did we find our Jerusalem? Do dreams fulfilled produce new ones? We drove past what used to be no-man's land and parked next to the wall facing one of the gates. I think Dov was talking, telling me 1948 war stories—he fought on the Jerusalem front and knew every stone and alley. I wasn't listening. I wasn't even looking. Jaffa gate, Shechem gate, flowers' gate, the Lions' gate, the Temple Mount, the Wall. I was almost surprised to find that "The Wailing Wall" was a real wall. Somehow I expected it to be an abstract container of tears, prayers of generations floating in midair, a tune of music hovering over a marked spot. But the wall was a wall, grey with age and smooth with touch, flowers sprouting from its cracks. There were shapes and real beauty of carved stones and colors and arches. I didn't notice reality and all I knew was one big abstract emotion of, "We are here. In the old city of Jerusalem."

I looked at faces and didn't see them. I looked at road signs and couldn't read. My fingers shyly felt the smooth old stones and didn't sense it. It was beyond words, beyond sensations, beyond me and Dov and the armed soldiers who walked amazed in the alleys. We drove to Jericho, the Dead Sea, Kalia. Childhood memories, refugees crossing the bridge to return to Jordan. Jericho grapes and red flame trees, the main square, the shut doors, soldiers resting. I refused to digest it. It was too early. It was not quite going abroad on a sight-seeing tour, neither was it a familiar home revisited. It lay between the curiosities and excitement, between Joshua and the Security Council decision, and I couldn't take it in. I wanted to return to the Sinai. We drove on to Bethlehem, the Church of the Nativity, the market, souvenir shops. My nervousness grew. Yesterday there were blood and fear and pride and victory. Today were the visitors from the rear shopping for camels carved in wood, poking their noses into courtyards of private dwellings, exclaiming at the low prices, pushing, sweating, collecting impressions and goods as if they deserved them. I struggled between shame and acceptance. It was normal, it was natural, but somehow not yet the time. I would have liked it all locked up for a while, quiet and respected, to have been given the chance to resume slowly a pace of normal life and only gradually introduce to it the seekers of half-priced vegetables and embroidery. Here the magic was gone. I entered the tomb of Rachel. I was pushed in to find myself crowded among orthodox men dressed in black praying and thanking and pleading—their names scribbled coarsely over the whitewashed walls. They were thanking God, and I was thanking the Yorams and the Uris, and I struggled out. Please let's go somewhere, anywhere quiet. We drove up the road to Mount Scopus, and Old Jerusalem lay below us like a gift. Holy and mysterious, walled in and expanding out, merging with the hills and reflecting the setting sun. It was Dov's city, and now I loved it. Like that, from above, in the silence of the hills of Judea with the complete inability to conceive of what happened. On the way back Dov asked me to marry him. I don't think I answered then. I was too full of questions to be able to answer anything.

We were to meet the division in its new home, Bir-Gafgafa, and before we left I asked Arik what he desired. "A salami sausage the length of a helicopter and Camembert cheese." They don't make sausages helicopter length, but I figured a few combined may make it. The cheese was obtained, too, some cakes and sweets, cigars, a bottle of wine, and we were on the road south again. My miserable mood changed as soon as we left Gaza and were back on the road to El-Arish where we arrived late at night.

I left Dov and a couple of visitors we had and went to look for Kuti. Somehow, I believed his face would erase the images that kept floating up—youngsters killed or wounded, children's faces when told "Father will not be back," mothers in black. The driver was scared. He was told sniping was still a danger in El-Arish and the silence and calm of the Arab city added to his fear. His was the only case of fright I've come across during the war. Mosques, trees in blossom, ruined roads, the airport, a few headlights, and back to headquarters where Kuti waited. We didn't talk much. He offered us some food and we listened to a radio broadcast. I was given a blanket and a room with a sofa and lay awake listening to soldiers' talk. They were leaving with dawn, they were reservists going home, to the workshops, desks, wives, and children. To the farms and the banks and civilian clothes. In a few days they'd be sitting in cafés telling of "their war" and remembering it with the nostalgia of a reservist. When the wife complains of dust they will say "You should have been in Um-Katef," and when they meet a stranger in the street who says shalom they will think, "We probably met during the war. I wonder what his name is." Tomorrow they'll tell their sons anecdotes and somewhere underneath there will be stories and memories they will never tell or discuss. In a few weeks they'll complain that the taxes are too high and shout at pedestrians or at drivers. They will think the load of soda-bottles crate too heavy, forgetting the weight of a bazooka, and they'll swear at the laundry when a shirt is returned with a button missing. They climbed the busses and trucks, some smiling, some sad, others singing. They were going home, to be what they were before —regular citizens.

In the morning we drove to Bir-Gafgafa. The corpses, fewer of them, were still rotting along the road in a frequency of telephone poles, but I welcomed the space, the absence of people, the heat, the desert wind. Bir-Gafgafa was somehow more pleasant than Nahel and it boasted a large airport with several runways, shelters and five hit and burned enormous Russian helicopters. They were the largest we'd seen, MI-6 type, I believe, and the skeleton of their propellers looked like oversized spiders. The metal debris around them was almost beautiful, like a new type of garden, silver and black H. G. Wells plants, almost alive.

The division had just arrived from Nahel and we found a place for a camp. The trailer was cleaned again and tents erected. We were settling in as if for a long, long stay. I sliced the salami sausage and produced the Camembert and bottle of wine—slightly above the required room temperature—and took the jeep for a drive. The prisoners from Nahel now had local prisoners for company. Some of them walked without water for a few days and fainted when captured—and the doctors had a full-time job on their hands. Other prisoners were working—digging or constructing or burying the dead, and those captured in Nahel were in better shape now. The patrols were looking for more of them for humanitarian reasons, helping direct them to a source of water and saving them from death by thirst and starvation.

106

The papers announced our casualties—679 dead and 2,563 wounded. Of them 255 badly, the others—light wounds. The talks in the trailer were different now. We were not offering final solutions, we were still arguing, but we agreed about some things. It was clear that the previous phase was over. The previous borders and the armistice agreements were annulled by the war. The new reality in the Middle East presented Israel as the strongest element, and as such it can talk a different language and had to be talked to differently.

"Jerusalem is beyond discussion," we said. We said, we felt, we meant. It will remain united and no decision or agreement can again deprive the capital of its Eastern limb and the holy places. Arik was now commander of the whole area and our headquarters was to handle all official visitors. The first one was my father. He arrived with a group of staff officers in a helicopter. Wearing khaki, tanned, smiling, he was surrounded by men with whom he worked and fought for tens of years. Eizer Weitzman—chief of operations and famous for years of brilliant command of the air force, Zvi Tsur—former chief of staff, Gandi, Shaike—commander of the south, Moti Hod—Commander of the air force, Amos, Man, and Arik. There was something homogeneous about this group of men. They were tough but they had a smile in their eyes. They would sacrifice everything but they cared for a flower, a poem, a piece of land. They were not politicians but they knew what it was all about and they were leaders. They were the men who, as Arik put it, say "follow me" rather than "forward," and this heritage they gave a whole army and its commanders—to the last section leader. They argued, at times they quarreled, sometimes they gossiped and turned against one another, but what united them was stronger than all—a devotion which knew no limit, an ability to compromise for the common good, and a sense of confidence in the physical and moral strength and superiority of the nation and its army.

They walked to the war room and Arik, aided by maps, explained the division's action during the war. My father offered me a ride to the Canal. We flew just above the road looking at the destroyed convoys along it. The air force and armor men were dividing the credit, exclaiming, "This one is ours," "That's a tank's hit." And we landed a mile or so away from the Suez Canal. If Jerusalem inspired me in the total historical emotional sense, here the inspiration was political. Ismaelia was bathed in red poinciana trees and I said to my father, "Look, how beautiful!" "And if it weren't beautiful, it would be as important," his answer was. We sat on a small bridge in Kantara, our feet dangling in the water. He told the other officers to join us. "Our feet in the water of the Suez Canal," he said. "Isn't that something!" The blue water was waveless. A large Polish airlines sign offered trips to Warsaw and a corpse floated toward us in the water. A Red Cross flag was waved to indicate another transport of prisoners to the other side. They, too, were going home. We evacuated after selection as many as we could. Thousands of them crossed here, scared of what their fate would be once they returned. They were not met as war heroes, and parades of women and children carrying flowers and cakes did not line their route. They were going home, true, and I hoped a mother and wife would tend them and be glad to see them alive, but what a country to be going back to. My father said, "It must be unbearable to be a part of a defeated army," and one of the commanders added, "What a fortunate state for an army to have never known defeat." Soldiers applauded the group I was with when we approached the helicopter. Arik and I left them in Bir-Gafgafa and I went to the kitchen tent to prepare a meal. Arik was spoiled by now and didn't regard our cold K-rations' meal in Kantara a serious one.

A few days passed. The events that marked our days had to do with a few incidents with still-retreating enemy platoons, reports of patrols, visits, and debates. If Jerusalem was beyond debating, it still left a large number of subjects to argue about. There was the Sinai—wilderness, perhaps, but it bordered on the Canal and had oil and manganese. It had Mount

Sinai and Sharm-El-Sheikh, it controlled the sea traffic between Asia, and Europe, and Africa. There was the west bank of the Jordan, fully populated but enjoying the natural border of the river Jordan. The heights of Syria with their preventive importance—artillery fire was no more a daily danger to lives and property of the valley settlements. There was the Gaza Strip, an annexed unnatural part of Egypt populated mostly by the refugees, and there was the refugee problem. No one answer or solution could be given to all areas, but one thing was clear to all of us—the price we were to demand for returning the new areas, or some of them, could not be less than the one thing we were after—peace. And until negotiations of peace commence, we could carry on as we did now. Strategically, those new frontiers gave us an advantage, economically they were a burden and a tremendous undertaking which we believed we could cope with, politically. We were beyond the position when any amount of pressure exercised on us made us jump. "We fought the war alone, we may have to fight the political war alone as well," people were saying, and it was not going to be easy. The old frontiers were gone and history presented us with the chance of reshaping the country guided by justice and interests. We were not going to miss that chance.

Egypt was rearming itself, France did not remove the embargo on shipments of arms to Israel, ships were stuck in the Canal's entrance, and Egypt refused to operate the Canal as long as we had its eastern bank, which meant a rise in petrol's transport fees, having to do an African detour to reach Britain and Europe. Internally our situation was not clean cut either. Will the emergency government continue to act? Will the labor movements unite? Will leadership be improved, and what will be the declared policy concerning the new areas? Sometimes it was like a new game. We were in the trailer enjoying dinner when someone would say, "Suppose it were demilitarized," meaning the ex-Jordanian west bank, or supervised by the U.N. or autonomous, or annexed, and we would proceed to examine each of the possibilities—the pros and the cons. I didn't give it much thought then. I hoped we'd not give up anything for less than a permanent agreement which would enable us to exist in peace. I also feared that we'd always be foreigners in the area to an extent and at best friction would take the place of armed conflict, friction of cultures, of backgrounds, religions, attitudes—friction which might in the long run be constructive.

Visiting journalists added their own opinions. We were reluctant to entertain them but also felt a certain responsibility. Public opinion became a major aspect of the political war and although the prewar and combat period produced a certain xenophobia in us we did spend many hours with correspondents and TV people patiently answering their questions.

Civilians from the rear arrived on visits. What for us was routine for them was a novelty. They looked at the Russian helicopters, the damaged roads, the prisoners, the war room as if they were participating in a battle.

I slept in the Lark most nights and turned the front seat into a cupboard. Mail and papers arrived, Yoske's canteen sold cold drinks and cigarettes, I was driving the jeep in the camp's area, and all I wanted was never to leave, never to face the daily routine of my "other life," never to lose the freedom of lack of possessions, lack of responsibilities other than to show a few people around or tend the kitchen. Several nights I found myself crying, almost unwillingly. Shaul asked, "Are you crying for one or for many?" I didn't know. The many became one, the suspicions became certainty with announcement of funerals, and it was impossible not to accept the fact that some people one loved and cared for were alive no more. A few of the older officers said, "Strange, this seems to be the last war for me," and yet, they, too, wondered.

On June 18 some of us got the order to leave. Suddenly it was over. Arik packed his small rucksack and folded his two blankets. My things were to travel north in the Lark. Dov was talking to the airport control tower, checking on the time of departure. We said shalom and "See you next week in town," and if I had tears in my eyes they were attributed to the sandstorm. Arik, Dov, and I boarded the small helicopter. Thirteen days earlier, at eight-fifteen, Arik had said, "Nua-Nua, Sof," and the Centurions crossed the frontier toward everything that was unknown. And now, thirteen days later, we were returning to all that was supposed to be familiar and homelike—as strangers. "Fly low to El-Arish and follow the beach as low as you can," Arik told the pilots. We were sitting and watching the scenery through the open side of the helicopter. The road, Gebel-Libni, El-Arish, the palm trees, and the beach. The white sands of Rafah, the camps near Gaza, the feminine curve of the shore line, the beauty of an untouched coast and dunes. Arik tried to shout above the helicopter's noise. He was stretching one hand as if showing us the view, as if we hadn't noticed it, and murmuring something. On a piece of paper—as it was obvious we couldn't hear—he wrote, "All this is ours," and he was smiling like a proud boy. When we crossed the old nonexistent border the scenery changed. No border stones need mark the difference. The land was now green and cultivated, the houses indicated a modern existence, tractors and combines were growing and harvesting, and girls in bikinis waved to us from the beaches.

Ashkelon, Ashdod, Jaffa and Tel-Aviv. For a brief moment I envied those girls. It must be wonderful for a soldier to meet his girl—wearing a dress, clean, a touch of perfume perhaps, a hair-do, a handbag—something to come back to. There I was. Dirt and dust, a silly braid uncombed for days, burned rough skin, heavy boots, red eyes. We landed and drove to Zahala in silence. Were we all thinking of tomorrow morning? By coincidence Arik met his wife Lilly on the road. He joined her and we drove behind their car. She rested her head on his shoulder. He was home. "All will be well," Dov promised me. "Home" now was something new, safer, larger, stronger, and happier.

About the Author

Yaël Dayan, born and raised in Israel, is the daughter of General Moshe Dayan, her country's Minister of Defense. A proficient linguist, a world traveler, and a journalist who reported from Vietnam for one of Israel's major papers, Miss Dayan is best known as a novelist. Her first novel, *New Face in the Mirror*, written during her army service, was a bestseller in 1960, and was translated into fourteen languages. Her next two books, *Envy the Frightened* and *Dust*, were written in Greece. Her latest novel, *Death Had Two Sons* (being published simultaneously with *Israel Journal*), was on press in the summer of 1967, when Miss Dayan flew back to Israel to rejoin the army. She was subsequently promoted to full lieutenant. She was recently married to Colonel Dov Sion.